Voodoo Dolls in Magick and Ritual

Denise Alvarado

Copyright © 2009 Denise Alvarado, All rights reserved.

Voodoo Dolls in Magick and Ritual, Copyright © 2009 Denise Alvarado, All rights reserved. No part of this publication may be reproduced or transmitted in any form or by any means, electronic, or mechanical, including photocopy, or any information storage and retrieval system, without permission from the author and publisher, except in brief quotations embodied in critical articles and reviews.

All artwork and photography is by Denise Alvarado or in the public domain.

Other books by this author:

The Voodoo Hoodoo Spellbook

A Guide to Serving the Seven African Powers

Voodoo Dolls in Magick and Ritual

A Guide for Invoking the Divine Power of Exu

A Pictorial Guide to Voodoo Dolls

The Gypsy Magic Spellbook

Contents

CHAPTER 1: 3
The History of Voodoo Dolls 3
    The History of Voodoo 5
    Creole Voodoo 8
    Voodoo Dolls 10
CHAPTER 2: 15
A Survey of Dolls and Ritual Effigies 15
    Venus of Willendorf 17
    Corn Dollies 20
    The Wicker Man 21
    Kachina Dolls 23
    African Ndebele Dolls 24
    Nkisi 25
    Bocio 26
    Fetishes 27
    Poppets 28
    Greek Kolossoi 28
CHAPTER 3: 30
Types of Voodoo Dolls 30
    Heirloom Dolls 32
    Voodoo Moss Dolls 34
    Swamp Witch Voodoo Dolls 34
    Voodoo Love Dolls 35
    Louisiana Broom Dolls 35
    Ju Ju Dolls 35
    Voodoo Devotional Dolls 36
    Voodoo Rope Dolls 37

Voodoo Bone Dolls	37
Corn Husk Dolls	37
Voodoo Wedding Dolls	38
Voodoo Hexing Dolls	39
Haitian Vodou Dolls	40
Wanga Dolls	42
Harlequin Dolls	42
CHAPTER 4:	75
How to Make a Voodoo Doll	75
Materials	77
Directions	78
CHAPTER 5: How to Make a Voodoo Poppet	84
Color Symbolism for Poppets	84
Poppet Patterns	85
Basic Poppet Pattern #1	86
Basic Poppet Pattern #2	87
Poppet Pattern #3: Mermaid	88
Poppet Pattern #4: Mermaid	89
Directions for Basic Stitches	90
Blanket Stitch	90
Running Stitch	91
How to Sew a Voodoo Poppet	92
More Ways to Make Poppets	101
Wax Poppets	101
Root Poppets	101
Clay Poppets	102
Wood Poppets	102
Paper Poppets	102
CHAPTER 6:	103
How to Make a Paper Voodoo Doll	103
Symbols for Drawing or Pasting on Paper Voodoo Dolls	103
Paper Voodoo Doll Patterns	104
Paper Voodoo Doll Pattern #1	106
Mandrake Poppet Doll Pattern #2: Female	107
Mandrake Poppet Doll Pattern #3: Male	108
Paper Voodoo Doll Pattern #4: Mermaid	109
CHAPTER 7:	110
How to Prepare your Voodoo Doll for Ritual Use	110
Clearing	111
Creation	112

 Consecration 113
  Step One 114
  Step Two 114
 Baptism 115
  How to Baptize a Voodoo Doll 115
CHAPTER 8: 117
Voodoo Doll Magick 117
 Principals of Image Magick 117
 How to Use a Voodoo Doll 120
  Use Your Voodoo Doll as a Focusing Tool 123
  Use Your Voodoo Doll as a Therapeutic Tool 123
  Use Your Voodoo Doll for Revenge 124
 Can You Really Kill Someone with a Voodoo Doll? 124
CHAPTER 9: 127
The Meaning of the Seven Pins 127
 Where to Stick It 128
 Karmically Incorrect Use of the Seven Pins 129
CHAPTER 10: 130
Spells and Rituals 130
 BANISH, BIND, AND ENEMY BE GONE 130
  Spell to Bind Someone Dangerous 131
  Banishment and Equalizer Spell 132
  Keep a Big Man Down Spell 134
  A Simple Ritual for Chango 135
  Voodoo Doll Banish and Hex Spell 136
 SPELL TO DOMINATE 136
 GAMBLER'S SPELL 137
 GOSSIP SPELLS 138
  Shut Your Mouth Spell 138
  Slippery Elm Banish Gossip Voodoo Doll Spell 139
 HEALING SPELLS 139
  Assyrian Healing Doll Spell 140
  Basic Voodoo Doll Healing Spell with Pins 141
  Yoruban Babaluye Healing Oil 141
 SPELL FOR JUSTICE 142
  Psalm 7 (King James Version) 142
 LOVE AND ATTRACTION SPELLS 144
  Commanding Doll Spell 144
  Love Drawing Voodoo Doll Spell 145
  Love Effigies 145

- Oshun Love Spell 145
- Oshun Love and Prosperity Spell 146
- New Orleans Voodoo Knot Doll Love Spell 147
- Pierced Heart Doll Spell 148
- Twenty Seven Day Paper Voodoo Doll Spell 148
- Voodoo Virility Doll Spell 149
- Wax Doll Summoning Spell 151
- Poppet Bonding Spell 151

WEALTH AND PROSPERITY SPELLS 152
- Mo' Money Spell 152
- Money Doll 152
- Wealth and Prosperity Voodoo Doll Spell 153

VOODOO DOLL CURSES 153
- Basic Pins and Needles Voodoo Doll Hex 154
- Death Curse 154
- Magic Doll Spell from the Great Book of St. Cyprian 155
- Voodoo Doll Curse from the Necronomicon 156
- Voodoo Doll Curse Herbal Blend Recipe 157
- To Cross an Enemy 157
- To Keep a Person Frustrated and Unsuccessful 158

CHAPTER 11: 160
Using the Psalms in Voodoo Doll Magick 160
- Psalm for Successful Business 160
  - Psalm 8 (King James Version) 161
- Psalm to Stop Persecution 161
  - Psalm 11 (King James Version) 162
- Psalm to Stop all Libel 162
  - Psalm 35 (King James Version) 163
- Psalm to Make Yourself Beloved 165
  - Psalm 47 (King James Version) 165
- Psalm to Make Your Home Lucky 165
  - Psalm 61 (King James Version) 166
- Psalms for Making Peace between Husband and Wife 166
  - Psalm 45 (King James Version) 167
  - Psalm 46 (King James Version) 168
- Psalm for Safe Travel at Night 169
  - Psalm 121 (King James Version) 169
- Psalm for Severe Headache or Backache 169
  - Psalm 3 (King James Version) 170
- Psalm for a Repentant Liar 170

  Psalm 132 (King James Version) 170
CHAPTER 12: 172
Prayers to Use when Petitioning the Spirits with Voodoo Dolls 172
  Eleggua / Elegua/Papa Legba 173
    Prayers for Saint Anthony 173
    Unfailing Prayer to Saint Anthony 174
  Obatalá 174
    Prayer to our Lady of Mercy 174
  Yemayá 175
    Prayer to Yemayá 176
  Oyá 176
    St. Theresa of the Child Jesus 176
  Oshun / Ochum 177
    African Prayer to Oshun 177
  Chango / Shango / Xango / Sango 177
    Prayer to Saint Barbara 177
  Ogun / Ogum 178
    Litany of Saint Anthony of Padua 178
  Orunla/ Orunmila/Orula 180
    Prayer to Saint John the Evangelist 180
  Babalú-Ayé 180
    Prayer to Saint Lazarus 181
  General Prayers 181
    Our Father 181
    Hail Mary 181
    Apostle's Creed 182
    Prayer to the Seven African Powers 182
CHAPTER 13: 183
Cursed Voodoo Dolls 183
  What Does a Cursed Voodoo Doll Look Like? 183
  How to Get Rid of a Cursed Voodoo Doll 186
    White Bath for Purification 187
  Voodoo Doll Reversal Spells 187
CHAPTER 14: 189
Recipes for Magickal Oils 189
  Bend-Over Oil 189
  Black Arts Oil 190
  Command and Compel Oil 190
  Crossing Oil 191
  Crossing Powder 191

Fast Luck Oil 191
Revenge Oil 191
Final Thoughts 193
Suppliers 195
Bibliography 198

Photos

Photo: 1. Portrait of Marie Laveau: Franck Schneider, Marie Laveau, c. 1920s, oil on canvas, Louisiana State Museum, Baton Rouge, Louisiana. 9
Photo: 2. Mammy doll from New Orleans. 16
Photo: 3. The Venus of Willendorf. Photo by Mathias Kabel, 2007. 18
Photo: 4. Examples of Voodoo dolls without feet, compared to the Venus of Willendorf. The two dolls on the left are believed to be cursed Voodoo dolls with their feet removed; the third photo is Venus; the fourth is the bottom of a New Orleans Voodoo doll. 19
Photo: 5. Claidheach harvest corn dolly 21
Photo: 6. An 18th century illustration of a wicker man. 22
Photo: 7. Kachina dolls from the author's private collection. 24
Photo: 8. African Ndebele doll. 25
Photo: 9. This authentic African fetish was carved in the Congo from a single piece of Native wood. The costume is woven of straw and then carefully sewn onto the carving. This type of fetish is believed by its creators to have magical powers. It is used in ceremonies (especially male puberty rites) to ward off evil spirits and undesirable women. The male adults dress up in similar life size straw costumes and masks. This fetish is from the author's private collection. 27
Photo: 10. Witch with Voodoo poppet 29
Photo: 11. Wanga Paket, created by the author. 44
Photo: 12. Images on Indian Doctor's grave, Chilkat Alaska, 1895, Winter and Pond. 45
Photo: 13. Djab Voodoo doll, created by the author. 46
Photo: 14. Swamp Witch Voodoo doll on display at the New Orleans Voodoo Museum. 47
Photo: 15. Wedding Couple created by the author. 48
Photo: 16. Louisiana Fertility Broom Doll created by the author 49
Photo: 17. Fertility doll from Africa, New Orleans Museum of Art. 50
Photo: 18. Erzulie Freda, created by the author. 51
Photo: 19. Black Cat Ju Ju Doll created by the author. 52
Photo: 20. Voodoo Rope Doll created by the author. 53

Photo: 21. Ju Ju doll created by the author. 54
Photo: 22. Papa La Bas at the New Orleans Voodoo Museum, New Orleans, La. 55
Photo: 23. Voodoo doll made from chicken bones by the author. 56
Photo: 24. A New Orleans Voodoo doll geared towards tourists, from the author's private collection. 57
Photo: 25. Bound twin mandrake roots by the author. 58
Photo: 26. Voodoo Doll – "God to Help You Meet Girls." From the author's private collection. 59
Photo: 27. Vintage black Voodoo dolls from the author's private collection. 60
Photo: 28. The face of Ogun, Father of Technology. Voodoo doll by the author as seen on National Geographic's Taboo, 2008. 61
Photo: 29. Large Voodoo doll with poppet and mandrake doll baby, created by the author. 62
Photo: 30. Vintage Voodoo dolls at the New Orleans Voodoo Museum. 63
Photo: 31. Corn Husk Voodoo doll. 64
Photo: 32. Black corn dolly. 65
Photo: 33. Papa Legba Voodoo doll, Guardian of the Crossroads, created by the author. 66
Photo: 34. Gran Ibo, the Swamp Witch, created by the author. 67
Photo: 35. Very old Voodoo doll of unknown origin. From the author's private collection. 68
Photo: 36. Vintage Voodoo doll from Marie Laveau's House of Voodoo, New Orleans, La. The label states the doll is for "intuition." From the author's private collection. 69
Photo: 37. Plastic Voodoo doll baby from Martinique, used as a cork. From the author's private collection. 70
Photo: 38. Haitian spirit bottle with Voodoo doll baby. 71
Photo: 39. Here is a novel Voodoo hexing doll made in the likeness of Ted Thompson, general manager for the Green Bay Packers. He is called "Voodoo Ted", and comes with his own cheesehead hat, rope, and pins. Designed for BluBanana by the author. 72
Photo: 40. Dachu Voodoo doll souvenir. From the author's private collection. 73
Photo: 41. Swamp Granny hoodoo gator Voodoo doll created by the author. Evil eye bead by Bountiful Bonita. 74
Photo: 42. A cross made from two sticks forms the foundation of the Voodoo moss doll. 78
Photo: 43. Wrap the cross with moss 79
Photo: 44. Cross with full moss 79

Photo: 45. Basic Voodoo Moss Doll 80
Photo: 46. Voodoo doll face with black eyed peas for eyes 81
Photo: 47. Voodoo moss dolls. 83
Photo: 48. Blanket stitch 90
Photo: 49. Basic poppet pattern. 93
Photo: 50. Pattern is placed on top of leather. 93
Photo: 51. Pattern is pinned to leather to keep from sliding around. 94
Photo: 52. This pattern was cut out using pinking shears. 94
Photo: 53. Front and back sides of poppet. 95
Photo: 54. The two sides are sewn together. 96
Photo: 55. A small opening is left on one side of the poppet for stuffing. ... 97
Photo: 56. Poppet and Spanish moss. 98
Photo: 57. Stuffed poppet. 99
Photo: 58. Stuffed poppet with buttons sewn on for eyes. 100
Photo: 59. Cursed Voodoo doll. 184
Photo: 60. Cursed bride Voodoo doll. 185

Figures

Figure 1. Harlequin Voodoo doll stuffed with Spanish moss 42
Figure 2. Poppet Pattern #1 86
Figure 3. Poppet pattern #2 87
Figure 4. Poppet pattern #3 88
Figure 5. Poppet pattern #4 89
Figure 6. Blanket stitch 91
Figure 7. Running Stitch 92
Figure 8. Symbols for Use with Paper Voodoo Dolls 104
9. Paper Voodoo doll pattern 106
10. Female mandrake 107
11. Male mandrake 108
12. Mermaid (La Sirene) 109

Introduction

I set about writing this book in response to the sheer volume of requests from customers and clients who had purchased the ebook predecessor *How to Voodoo with Voodoo Dolls*. At first, I decided to transpose the ebook into print form; however, in the process of doing so, I realized that I had a lot more to say about the subject. As a result, this book is a completely rewritten and much expanded version of the ebook.

The information I present in this book is based on my personal perspective as an artist and mystic who was born and raised in the land of Voodoo - New Orleans, Louisiana. It is with this brand of Voodoo hoodoo that I am most familiar and so most of this book is written from this point of view. It is but one perspective, and though I attempt to be thorough, by no means do I claim this book to be the definitive guide to all things related to Voodoo dolls. It is, however, the first book that takes a serious look at Voodoo dolls within the context of history, as well as within the context of magick.

Much of the information contained in this book is drawn from folklore collections, oral tradition from family, friends, customers, medicine men and women, and healers over the span of a lifetime, recipes from 19th and 20th century formularies, historical accounts of slaves in the southern United States, objective evaluation of anthropological and psychological literature, art history, and from my personal grimoires. The information contained herein is strictly for educational purposes. Should you decide to put into practice any of the information contained in this book, I assume no responsibility for the results, whether positive or negative.

I hope you find this book an informative and enjoyable read about one of the most colorful and mystifying archetypes of spiritual expression – the Voodoo doll.

Blessings,

Denise Alvarado

CHAPTER 1:
The History of Voodoo Dolls

Mysterious and provocative, the foremost reigning icon of African derived religions in the minds of the Western world is the Voodoo doll. Standing at the crossroads as a psychic link between the world of Spirit and the world of the mundane, Voodoo dolls provide a frightening glimpse into the world of the supernatural. Images of ugly pin-sticking dolls used for hexing your neighbor and summoning evil spirits, satanic evil-doers engaging in bloody sacrifices, brain-eating zombies, rock music and drugs, sexual promiscuity and homosexuality, the occult and demonism, Voodoo and demonism--they all go together in the minds of the general public, thanks to Hollywood and sensational novels. Very few things have the potential to create as much fear, panic, and paranoia as the discovery of a Voodoo doll lying on the front steps of home sweet home.

But how threatening can a doll be? Using a Voodoo doll is not like holding a gun to someone's head, after all. On the other hand, Voodoo dolls are quite possibly worse, because to the uninformed they symbolize a war waged against your very soul. And, how can you defend yourself against that?

Voodoo Dolls

Using dolls and effigies in sympathetic magic rituals is as old as humankind. More often than not, ritual dolls and effigies were used for healing, fertility, and empowerment. In some cultures such as ancient Greece, they were used to bind enemies. European poppets were widely used in folk magic and witchcraft to curse an enemy. Other types of dolls were used in harvest customs and burial rites, made as talismans, or used as teaching aids for children.

Beyond the era of ancient dolls, Voodoo dolls as we know them today are created for many purposes. In New Orleans, which can be considered the contemporary hub of Voodoo dolls in America, they are created as gris gris (pronounced *gree gree*), a form of talismanic magick. The word *gris* means *grey*, denoting that which lies between black and white. Gris gris is both a noun and a verb, referring to a ritually prepared object such as a doll or a small cloth bag filled with magickal ingredients, as well as the act of working the gris gris (i.e. spell or charm). In New Orleans, there are four main categories of gris gris: love, power and domination, luck and finance, and uncrossing. These four categories are among the most commonly requested gris gris associated with Voodoo dolls.

Traditionally, Voodoo dolls are created to represent a deity or to house a spirit, not unlike the nkisi, statues of power used throughout the Congo Basin in Central Africa that are thought to contain spiritual powers or spirits. Although they are most commonly depicted as objects of revenge, most practitioners of Voodoo make a concerted effort to disassociate from the malevolent use of Voodoo dolls, which is considered a form of Bokor Voodoo or sorcery. Instead, Voodoo dolls are created and used for positive purposes. Approximately 90% of the use of Voodoo dolls is centered on healing, finding true love, and spiritual guidance. They are also used as focusing tools in ritual and meditation.

In New Orleans, Voodoo dolls are largely sold as souvenirs, curios, and novelty items. There are literally hundreds of kinds of voodoo dolls available; most are mass produced in Taiwan for the tourist trade, but many are created by local practitioners. These dolls can usually be identified by their similarities to each other, and often come with a packet of pins and instructions. For the most part, people who purchase a Voodoo doll will keep it around as a warm and fuzzy reminder of New Orleans, the Land of Voodoo.

So how did we get from objects of empowerment, spirituality, and souvenir to evil minions of hell? To answer this question requires a brief jaunt into the sociopolitical history of our country.

The History of Voodoo

Voodoo[1] has been hailed as quite possibly the oldest religion known to humankind, originating some 7,000 years ago. The word voodoo means "spirit" or "mystery." Voodoo believers accept the existence of one god (*Bon Dieu* or *Good God*), below which are the powerful spirits referred to as *loa*. These powerful spirits are responsible for the daily matters in life in the areas of family, love, money, happiness, wealth, and revenge. The loa are not that different from the Saints of Catholicism and angels in Christianity in that the

---

[1] There are a number of different ways to spell Voodoo. I have chosen to use the spelling Vodou to denote the religion as it is practiced in Haiti, Vodun to denote the religion as it is practiced in Africa, and Voodoo, as it is practiced in New Orleans.

loa are not prayed to; rather, they are asked to intercede with God on our behalf.

During the Diaspora, African slaves brought Vodun with them to plantations in Brazil, Haiti, Cuba, and Louisiana where it blended with regional indigenous spiritual and healing practices, European folk magic, and elements of Catholicism. The resulting religious traditions are referred to as *African derived religions*. Among the most well known African derived religions are Santería, which is practiced in Cuba and in many parts of the United States, Vodou, which is practiced in Haiti and in parts of the United States, and Creole Voodoo, as it is known in New Orleans, Louisiana.

There are conflicting accounts regarding the evolution of Creole Voodoo in Louisiana. By some accounts, the slave population came to New Orleans by way of Haiti; however, according to local historians, the African slave trade came directly to the New World to Louisiana in order to avoid pirating of the slaves. Most Africans were captured from many different tribes throughout West Africa, including the kingdom of Dahomey, which occupied parts of today's Togo, Benin and Nigeria. These slaves brought their religious beliefs and spirits with them. Though tribal customs and religions differed, they shared several common core beliefs, such as ancestor worship, the use of singing, drumming and dancing in religious rituals, the use of crude wooden figures in magic, and spirit possession. For many enslaved Africans, such spiritual traditions and practices provided them with fundamental psychological and emotional coping mechanisms for their unimaginable suffering.

In 1782, the governor of Louisiana outlawed the importation of black slaves from the West Indies. He believed they were a threat to the citizen's safety because of their practice of Voodoo. As white colonists became outnumbered by the sheer volume of Africans in captivity, the governor sought to prohibit the practice of Voodoo because he was afraid that it may fuel a slave uprising.

Indeed, Voodoo became one of the primary ways for slaves to resist the oppression of their slave owners. The warrior gods sustained and empowered them, and assisted in their ultimate liberation from slavery. For example, the success of the Haitian revolution against the French is attributed in large part to the help of special Voodoo spirits called *djabs*. Legend has it that the Haitian revolution of 1791 began with the Bwa Caiman ceremony led by a Vodou priest named Boukman. During this ceremony, everyone who was present committed to the fight for freedom after the spirit Ezili Dantor came and received a black pig as an offering. Djabs were invoked by Haitian slaves to fight along side them in battle. These spirits are believed to have provided protection against bullets, and to have used biological warfare in the form of yellow fever to ultimately wipe out most of General LeClerc's military force. As a result, the Haitian people were liberated from their French masters in 1804, and the first and only Black People's Republic in the Western hemisphere was established.

Voodoo was demonized as a savage religion and actively suppressed during colonial times. Priests and followers were murdered and their shrines and paraphernalia were destroyed because of the threat they posed to Christianity. Slaves were forcibly baptized into the Roman Catholic Church upon arrival to Haiti and America. This forced the followers to go underground to worship their deities and venerate their ancestors. Ironically, Catholicism proved to be an effective shroud for continuing Voodoo, as some elements such as the saints, were compatible with the indigenous spirits of the African pantheon. Ingeniously, the African slaves worshipped under the guise of Catholicism and the syncretized new Voodoo survived.

Four hundred years following the Diaspora, the Voodoo religion remains a central part of spiritual life for millions of people living in Haiti, West Africa, and to a lesser extent in the United States. For example, merchants in the African open-air markets sell voodoo talismans known as "fetishes" alongside other basics of life. Statues representing Voodoo spirits, dried animal heads and other animal parts, are sold for their medicinal properties and their spiritual power. In Haiti, an estimated 70 percent of Haiti's 8.8 million people practice Vodou to some extent, including many who claim to be Catholic or another religion. In April of 2003, the Haitian government officially sanctioned Vodou as a state religion. As well, an estimated 15% of the population New Orleans practiced some form of Voodoo prior to hurricane Katrina.

Creole Voodoo

In 1809, Napoleon invaded Spain forcing thousands of people to flee to Cuba. Around this time, approximately 10,000 Haitian and Cuban refugees arrived in New Orleans, bringing with them their own Vodou traditions to add to the African traditions already practiced in New Orleans.

During these formative years of Creole Voodoo, several notable root doctors and Voodoo Queens emerged. These included Doc Ya Ya, Madame Titite, Bayou John, Don Pedro, Sanité Dédé, and Marie Saloppé. However, the most famous and influential of all of these was Marie Laveau (see photo 1).

According to Luiseh Teish (1985), Marie Laveau was responsible for doing three things that maintained the authenticity of Voodoo in New

Orleans. First, she combined the worship of Voodoo gods with Catholic Saints. For example, St. Peter was Legba, St. Michael was Blanc Dani, and St. John was Chango. Second, she standardized the rituals and paraphernalia of Voodoo. According to Teish (1985),

> Friday night became altar night. St. John's Eve was the annual ritual. Candles, dolls, conjure bags and balls were dispensed for every occasion. (Teish, 1985, p. 179).

The third thing Marie Laveau did for Creole Voodoo was turn it into a legitimate business. People could purchase any number of services, dolls, or gris gris for a price. Moreover, people gladly paid anywhere from ten to thousands of dollars for one of her charms. In addition to these three things, Marie Laveau was responsible for rekindling the memory of the Rainbow Serpent (Damballah Wedo), known as the Great Zombi in New Orleans.

Photo: 1. Portrait of Marie Laveau: Franck Schneider, Marie Laveau, c. 1920s, oil on canvas, Louisiana State Museum, Baton Rouge, Louisiana.

When Marie Laveau reached her seventies, it is said that she retired and surrendered her title to her daughter, Marie Laveau II, who carried on the traditions of her mother. Both Maries are said to be buried in the infamous family crypt in St. Louis Cemetery No. 1, along with their mother and father.

After a time, Voodooists geared towards a more original and independent Voodoo with less structure. Many queens and kings tended to their own congregations. However, their remains some consistent characteristics of Creole Voodoo such as Papa La Bas the Trickster (Papa Legba), divination, herbalism, the importance of elders, funerals, ancestor worship (Teish, 1985), elements of Catholicism, gris gris, and Voodoo dolls.

Voodoo Dolls

Among the slave population in Louisiana during the 18th and 19th centuries, image magick using dolls was commonplace. *Image magick* is a type of magick based on the concept of *like attracts like* and is discussed in greater detail in the chapter *Voodoo Doll Magick*. Archaic dolls bound with cat gut or twine and stuck with pins or fish bones have been discovered on several Louisiana plantations. Some of these figural forms found among the slave population bore a striking resemblance to the bocio of Africa. The bocio figurines were aesthetically provocative empowerment objects produced primarily in the lower Western Africa regions of Benin and Togo. These figures were artistic assemblages as well as magickal objects, and would often have a variety of items attached to the figure. For example, personal items, cloth, rope, nails or tacks were driven into the figure to activate its power and invoke the spirit. According to Moreau de Saint Méry (1797), the Africans "believed in magic and that the power of their fetiches have followed them across the sea…Little rude figures of wood or stone, representing men or animals, are for them things of supernatural power, and they call them *garde corps* (body guards). There are a number of Negroes who acquire absolute power over others by this means" (Herskovitz, 1964, p. 221).

The bocio figurines were more than just scary looking magickal objects; they served a psychotherapeutic role as well. Traditionally, bocio were created in response to specific needs, and were believed to help people influence events in their lives for positive or negative ends. For example, bocio may be constructed for protection from illness, safety on the road, to promote success in economic matters, or fertility. It is easy to envision some of the reasons bocio may have been created and employed by slaves. For example, they may have been used for protection from abuse and brutality, safety for the family, revenge for abuse suffered at the hands of their masters, and/or to promote freedom from bondage. Obviously, bocio were a powerful means for psychological catharsis, as well as an effective tool for empowerment in the context of social and political crisis.

Like modern day Voodoo dolls, the process of creating a bocio was an empowering activity and sometimes involved more than one person. For example, there was the artist who created the raw figure, the diviner who activated the object by attaching a variety of personal items to the sculpture, and the client who uses it in a particular ritual context (Blier, 1995). Sometimes one person completed all three steps, which may have resulted in an enhanced sense of empowerment for that individual.

In Haiti, another form of doll emerged that may have taken the place of the more threatening bocio. Cloth dolls were created and brought to cemeteries to activate their power. Sometimes these cloth dolls were brought to cemeteries and nailed to a tree with an old shoe and an attached message to act as messengers to the spirit world.

Voodoo Dolls

In the process of conducting research for writing this book, I came across only one study on the topic of Voodoo dolls; specifically, this was a survey of Voodoo dolls in antiquity (see Faraone, 1988). This examination discovered 15 archaic Voodoo dolls in Greece, nine from Sicily and Italy, four from North Africa, seven from Egypt, three from the Near East, and one from the Black Sea (Ankarloo, et al. 1999). In ancient Greece, Voodoo dolls, known as Kolossoi, were found alongside curse tablets. These dolls are most frequently found in graves, sanctuaries, bodies of water, a riverbed, a sewer, and a Hellenistic house on Delos (Ankarloo, et al.).

A surprising number of ancient Voodoo dolls were fashioned out of lead or bronze. However, the evidence shows that wax was used in late ancient Egypt, and wax was used in conjunction with lead during the fourth century B.C. Other dolls were found to be created out of mud, clay, terra cotta, and possibly the dirt from graves (Graf, 1994). Many of these dolls are found with numerous nails stuck in them, similar to the bocio of African origin. In New Orleans, dolls were made from mud, clay, wax, cloth, sticks, and Spanish moss into which pins or fish bones would be stuck to activate the power of the gris gris.

The aforementioned survey of Voodoo dolls in ancient Greece and Rome clearly illustrates that the use of Voodoo dolls as a means of defense was not limited to African slaves in the New World. For example, slaves in ancient Greece are thought to have used Voodoo dolls to bind and curse those in positions of power. The fear of such magickal activity is reflected in the sentiment "the unutterable crime of the wicked public slave" when referring to the discovery of oblong coffins in a graveyard that contained Voodoo dolls with the names of town officials inscribed on its legs (Ankarloo, et al. 1999).

The use of Voodoo dolls in ancient Rome and Greece was not limited to cursing. For example:

> A doll made of dough is employed in a necromantic ritual recounted by Heliodorus (Aethipoica, 6.14). Horace's Canidia uses a doll made of wool, alongside one made of wax, for erotic purposes (Satires, 1.8.30; cf, Tupet, 1976, 44-50, 302). One of the accusations made of Apuleius under the charge that he practiced magic was that he worshipped with extravagant rites a skeleton-statue made of rare wood, and hailed it as "king" (Apology, 61.2; cf. Graf, 1994a, 96-8). (Ankarloo, et al. 1999, p.).

This very brief exploration of the history of Voodoo dolls reveals some universal characteristics of humanity that knows no temporal, cultural, or racial boundaries. Voodoo dolls are used in a similar fashion wherever they are found, although one culture may emphasize one purpose over another. In ancient Greece, binding and nailing Kolossoi is not that different from the binding and nailing of bocio in Africa. While these cultures are separated by thousands of years and thousands of miles, they were connected by trading and colonizing activities. How much influence one culture had on another with regards to Voodoo dolls in unclear; however, what is known about the contemporary Voodoo doll is that its cultural influences are many.

The Voodoo doll in Louisiana evolved during a time of great oppression and suffering. Its use as a defense mechanism by slaves permitted the symbolic unleashing of hate, humiliation, and suffering upon cruel slave masters without having to personally confront the slave master, which would have been extremely dangerous. Later, it was used as a principle tool in Marie

Voodoo Dolls

Laveau's standardization of the rituals and paraphernalia of Creole Voodoo. Voodoo dolls were considered evil by colonizers because it was assumed they were used to direct negative energy towards another person. At times perhaps they were, but can you blame slaves for coping in this manner? In truth, the concept of the evil Voodoo doll that continues to exist in the public psyche is a blatant result of slavery and early colonizers' attempts to dehumanize Africans and demonize their traditional religions. Criminalizing Voodoo then and demonizing Voodoo now feeds the collective shadow of the times, nurturing the essence of the African Diaspora and the very evil that drove it.

CHAPTER 2:
A Survey of Dolls and Ritual Effigies

The making of dolls, poppets, fetishes, and ritual effigies has taken place since antiquity. Human-like forms made of clay, stone, cloth, wax, roots, and wood meant to contain the essence or power of particular spirits can be found from early paleolithic cultures to contemporary society.

According to the available archaeological evidence, dolls are believed to be the oldest known toy. Dolls have been found in Egyptian tombs dating to as early as 2000 BC. In Egypt, as well as Greece and Rome, it was common to find dolls in the graves of children. Many were made of wood, although pottery dolls were buried with children from wealthier families. Dolls with movable limbs and removable clothing date back to 200 BCE.

In ancient times, dolls were used as representations of a deity, and played a central role in religious ceremonies and rituals. Effigies, for example, were used in religious rituals to represent an undesired person or spirit and burned to destroy the unwanted element. In traditional European pagan cultures, corn dollies were made of straw and associated with harvest customs. Native American Kachinas dolls were meticulously carved from

Voodoo Dolls

cottonwood root and painted to represent figures from Hopi mythology. Voodoo dolls are believed to be used by slaves as spiritual tools of empowerment and protection. In many early cultures, dolls were used for fertility purposes. Today, Voodoo dolls and poppets continue to be used in magick and ritual.

The first commercially available black dolls were made in Germany out of paper maché in the 1820s. Created as playthings for white children, they were dressed in subservient roles. The dolls produced from the 1800s to the 1960s included Aunt Jemima, Little Black Sambo, mammies, pickaninnies, and butlers (see photo 2). These dolls illustrate how whites viewed themselves as superior to African Americans, and how they believed African Americans accepted their maligned social status. Racist doll images permeated mass culture, having a profound effect on children as well as adults. People responded to these images by embracing them or rejecting them, and oftentimes, internalizing the messages underlying them.

Photo: 2. Mammy doll from New Orleans.

In the United States, doll-making became an industry in the 1860s, after the Civil War. In the 20th century, dolls depicting humans, animals, mythical creatures, and abstract beings, began to be accepted as fine art. Art dolls are now featured in modern art and fine art photography, shown in galleries, and placed on display at museums.

Voodoo dolls as we know them today do not have one particular origin; rather, they are the natural result of the melding of cultural influences that converged in the South. In the following section, we will take a look at some of the iconic, archetypal dolls that have made their mark in history and influenced in one way or another on the modern Voodoo doll.

Venus of Willendorf

One of the most famous of the early human-like effigies is the *Venus of Willendorf*, also known as the *Woman of Willendorf* (see photo 3).

This icon of prehistoric art is a female figurine estimated to have been created between 24,000 BCE – 22,000 BCE. It was discovered in 1908 by archaeologist Josef Szombathy in a village in Lower Austria near the city of Krems, a paleolithic site near Willendorf. It is carved from an oolitic limestone that is not local to the area, tinted with red ochre, and measures 4 3/8 inches. Because the figurine has no feet and is unable to stand on its own, it is speculated that she was meant to be held in the palm of the hand. The Venus is believed to be associated with fertility because of her exaggerated vulva, breasts, and swollen belly (Whitcomb, 2005).

Voodoo Dolls

Photo: 3. The Venus of Willendorf. Photo by Mathias Kabel, 2007.

The Venus of Willendorf is a worthy focus of the present discussion because some modern day Voodoo dolls share similar characteristics in their construction. For example, the Venus lacks facial features. This characteristic is significant because the face is considered a key aspect of human identity. But why wouldn't she have a face? Well, if her purpose was as a fertility object, then her face wasn't a key concern. Rather, it was those parts of the body that had to do with the conception and nurture of children that were important.

Similarly, Voodoo dolls sometimes lack facial features, or have very generic features. This enables the owner of the doll to focus on the purpose of the doll without being distracted by who or what the doll may look like. Also, a blank face provides the opportunity to personalize the doll by adding a photograph or other image of the person it may represent.

Another important feature of the Venus is her lack of feet (see Photo 4). It has been suggested that her creator made her that way in order to curb the figurine's power to leave wherever she had been placed. However, even if she had feet, it seems doubtful she was meant to stand up, given her size and the comfort in which she reportedly lays in the palm of one's hand.

Voodoo dolls crafted in the traditional New Orleans fashion also lack feet, as do some cursed Voodoo dolls; albeit, for different reasons. Some Voodoo dolls found in New Orleans lack feet due to the rudimentary nature of their construction. They are primitively created from two sticks that are formed into a cross and wrapped with Spanish moss. As such, their design doesn't lend itself to having feet. On the other hand, cursed Voodoo dolls often have their feet removed or are created without feet. This can be a metaphor for rendering a target immobile.

Finally, the Venus has uncharacteristically detailed hair for the time period in which she was created. She has seven concentric horizontal bands that encircle the head, with two more half-bands below at the back of her neck. The top circle is in the form of a rosette, and the bands resemble braids. While little is known about the significance of this feature in the context of paleolithic culture, in later cultures the number seven was regarded as a magic number (especially in New Orleans hoodoo), and hair was considered a source of strength, as well as the seat of the soul (Witcombe, 2005).

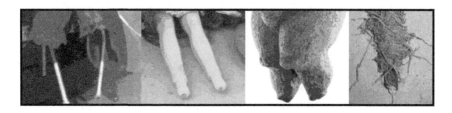

Photo: 4. Examples of Voodoo dolls without feet, compared to the Venus of Willendorf. The two dolls on the left are believed to be cursed Voodoo dolls with their feet removed; the third photo is Venus; the fourth is the bottom of a New Orleans Voodoo doll.

Corn Dollies

In traditional European pagan culture, corn dollies were made of straw and associated with harvest customs. Corn dollies were made from the last bit of corn to be harvested, and ploughed back into the ground in the spring during the first planting. It was believed that the spirit of the corn lived amongst the crops and harvesting it made it the corn spirit homeless. Thus, the corn dollies were a place where the corn spirit could reside during the winter after the harvest (see photo 5).

The harvest rituals associated with the Corn Mother and Corn Maiden are described by James George Frazer (1922):

> In the neighborhood of Danzig the person who cuts the last ears of corn makes them into a doll, which is called the Corn-mother or the Old Woman and is brought home on the last wagon. In some parts of Holstein the last sheaf is dressed in women's clothes and called the Corn-mother. It is carried home on the last wagon, and then thoroughly drenched with water. The drenching with water is doubtless a rain-charm. In the district of Bruck in Styria the last sheaf, called the Corn-mother, is made up into the shape of a woman by the oldest married woman in the village, of an age from 50 to 55 years. The finest ears are plucked out of it and made into a wreath, which, twined with flowers, is carried on her head by the prettiest girl of the village to the farmer or squire, while the Corn-mother is laid down in the barn to keep off the mice. In other villages of the same district the Corn-mother, at the close of harvest, is carried by two lads at the top of a pole. They march behind the girl who wears the wreath to the squire's house, and while he receives the wreath and hangs it up in the hall, the Corn-mother is placed on the top of a pile of wood, where she is the centre of the harvest supper and dance.—
> *The Golden Bough*, chapter 45

In Great Britain, corn dollies were typically crafted out of wheat, rye, barley, and oats. In Ireland, they were made out of rush, and in Southern

France, palm leaves. In New Orleans, an old style of Voodoo doll was made out of straw. Representations of the Ancient Roman goddess Ceres is said to have been made out of an entire sheath of wheat. Ceres is the goddess of growing plants (particularly cereals) and of motherly love. Today, Ceres is still worshipped in Religio Romana Neopaganism.

Photo: 5. Claidheach harvest corn dolly

The Wicker Man

The *Wicker Man* was a large wicker statue of a human allegedly used by the ancient Druids (priests of Celtic paganism) for human sacrifice by burning it in effigy (see photo 6). In modern times the figure has been adopted for festivals as part of some neopagan-themed ceremonies, notably without the human sacrifice element.

Wicker Men are set ablaze during some neopagan festivities. Typically, Celtic neopagans, Neo-druids, or Wiccans are those who use such a motif in their festivities because they, unlike other neopagan groups, are either inspired by, or follow a reconstructed form of, Celtic paganism. At other times, neopagans do not burn wicker men, but keep them as idols for protection, often merging them with the Green Man.

Photo: 6. An 18th century illustration of a wicker man.

Wicker men range from life sized to huge, humanoid, temporary sculptures that are set ablaze during a celebration, usually toward the end of the event. They are constructed with a wooden frame that is woven with flexible sticks such as willow. Some Wicker men are extremely complex and require days of construction.

Kachina Dolls

Kachinas dolls are stylized religious icons, meticulously carved from cottonwood root and painted to represent figures from Hopi mythology (see photo 7). Originally used to teach children about their religion, they have become a popular Hopi art form. The Hopi Indians use Kachina dolls to embody the characteristics of the powerful spirits of the earth, east, west, south, north, sky, and water. The dolls themselves are not seen as something to be worshipped, and technically they do not even depict sacred beings. Rather, they depict the Kachina dancers, men who wear Kachina masks during various Hopi ceremonies in imitation of the spirits.

In Hopi and Zuni tribes, kachina dolls are presented to the women and children of the tribe and are kept in the home as fetish objects. From about one-year old until they are ten, Hopi girls receive two dolls each year. They are presented to them during the Bean Dance and the Home Dance. The dolls are only given to the women because the women of the tribe do not possess the same degree of contact with the supernatural as the men of the tribe do. Therefore, the men who dance and impersonate the different Kachinas carve small wooden replicas of themselves and present them to infants and girls (Wright, 1977).

The Kachinas are ancestral spirits which act as intermediaries between humans and the gods. The identity of each Kachina is depicted by the specific shape of the mask, intricate use of color, and elaborate ornamentation with feathers, leather, and fabric. Each Kachina is also portrayed using distinct behavior, dance steps, gestures, and vocalizations.

Photo: 7. Kachina dolls from the author's private collection.

African Ndebele Dolls

While many people maintain that dolls have little to do with Voodoo, the opposite is actually true. In Africa, from whence Voodoo as we know it in the United States originates, doll fetishes and other power objects are a common aspect of the Vodun religion and culture. Dolls are created as objects laden with ritual and religious associations within the community.

For example, it is customary for men from the Ndebele tribe in Southern Africa to place special dolls outside young women's huts during courtship, indicating their intention to propose marriage (see photo 8). When she prepares for marriage, the young woman names and cares for the doll, and even names her first child after the doll. African dolls are also used as charms to insure fertility in women and in puberty rites for boys, and are used as teaching aids, for entertainment, as supernatural intermediaries, and are ritually manipulated for magickal purposes.

Photo: 8. African Ndebele doll.

Nkisi

A ***nkisi*** literally translates as "sacred medicine". The term nkisi is the general name for a variety of holy objects used throughout the Congo Basin in Central Africa thought to contain spiritual powers or spirits. Minkisi (plural) are primarily containers such as ceramic vessels, gourds, animal horns, shells, bundles, dolls, or any other object that can contain spiritually-charged substances. Minkisi are often referred to as portable graves because they may contain personal items of a powerful individual as one of the main ingredients. Even graves can be considered minkisi because they house the spirits of the dead.

Minkisi may be created for the protection and wellbeing of the community or for the private use of an individual, according to their specific needs. For example, individuals may need protection for themselves and their families, or seek general success in their economic pursuits. One of the most common purposes minkisi address is a woman's desire to conceive and prevent miscarriages.

Bocio

Throughout Africa, from the Gulf of Guinea to the Kongo Kingdom, are wooden carvings called ***bocio.*** These human figures were prevalent prior to and during the nineteenth century. Priests and diviners prescribe bocio to promote health and wellbeing. Similar to Voodoo dolls of today, bocio are created to address the needs of the person it is created for, such as securing a love relationship or protecting one's home and family. A bocio is activated when the individual attaches certain raw materials or personal items to the sculpture. Bocio are often bound with cords and sometimes pierced with nails or tacks. These objects predated the slave trade and functioned to ward off potential evil, among other things.

Fetishes

Theoretically, fetishism is present in all religions, but its use in the study of religion is derived from studies of traditional West African religious beliefs, as well as Voodoo, which is derived from those beliefs. The word *fetish* derives from the Portuguese word *feitiço*. A fetish is an object, talisman, or amulet, believed to have supernatural powers (see photo 9). The term was used by the Portuguese to refer to religious objects used by the African natives. These objects may have been used in sympathetic magic, identified in a dream, associated with good fortune, or according to Lang "they may (like a tree with an unexplained stir in its branches, as reported by Kohl) have seemed to show signs of life by spontaneous movements" (1900, p.147).

Photo: 9. This authentic African fetish was carved in the Congo from a single piece of Native wood. The costume is woven of straw and then carefully sewn onto the carving. This type of fetish is believed by its creators to have magical powers. It is used in ceremonies (especially male puberty rites) to ward off evil spirits and undesirable women. The male adults dress up in similar life size straw costumes and masks. This fetish is from the author's private collection.

Fetishes are also commonly used in Native American religion and culture. Small stone carvings are crafted to resemble animals with sacred qualities. For example, the bear may represent the shaman, the buffalo may represent the provider, the mountain lion may represent the warrior, and the wolf may symbolize the pathfinder.

Poppets

The word **poppet** is actually an older spelling of the word **puppet**, from the Middle English *popet*, meaning a small child or doll. *Poppet* is also an English term of endearment. Nowadays, the word *poppet* generally refers to its use in folk-magic.

In folk-magic and witchcraft, a poppet is a doll made to represent a person, for casting spells on that person. These dolls may be fashioned from such materials as a carved root, grain or corn shafts, a fruit, paper, wax, a potato, clay, branches, or cloth stuffed with herbs. The intention is that whatever actions are performed upon the effigy will be transferred to the subject as in sympathetic magic. If the spell is a curse, the poppet is worked in any number of ways, including piercing it with pins, nails or shards, binding it with cord, covering it with hot candle wax, or hanging it by the neck.

Poppets are often used for healing purposes, promoting health, finding love, creating happiness and good luck, for protection, for binding, cursing, and for manipulating energy in numerous other ways.

Greek Kolossoi

In ancient Greece, poppets called *Kolossos* (kaw-lawss-SAUCE) were typically made for defensive purposes. Their use was aimed at containing hostile forces or binding protective forces, warding off an invading enemy, or protecting one's home and family. The ancient Greek practice of constructing and using these ritual dolls dates from the fourth century BCE (Faraone, 1991).

Photo: 10. Witch with Voodoo poppet

CHAPTER 3:
Types of Voodoo Dolls

There are almost as many different kinds of Voodoo dolls as there are people making them on this planet. They differ in construction, materials, purpose, and artist interpretation. There are, however, some styles that have become the sort of standard over the years, defined by their purpose more than anything else. The most popular purposes for Voodoo dolls in New Orleans include: love; power and domination; good luck and prosperity; uncrossing, healing, fertility, protection, and connection with the Divine. Sometimes, Voodoo dolls are used for revenge when revenge is justified, as in cases of rape and murder.

The Voodoo doll can be considered a form of gris-gris. Gris gris is essentially a charm or amulet designed to bring something positive such as luck, love, or money to its possessor. Contrary to popular belief, Voodoo dolls are usually used for blessing and healing, as opposed to hexing and cursing. They are used as focusing tools, and through creative visualization just about any positive purpose can be accomplished. And yes, negative effects can be accomplished as well, if that is the will of the doll's creator or possessor. Most reputable Voodoo artisans and practitioners do not endorse

Types of Voodoo Dolls

the use of Voodoo dolls for negative purposes, though, and for good reason if you believe in karma or the "harm none, do what ye will" rede of the modern day Wiccan. In fact, the stereotypical pin-sticking evil little doll is more the creation of Hollywood than of reality. Unfortunately, this stereotype has persisted and contributed in a big way to the misunderstanding of Voodoo as a whole.

Today, as in the past, Voodoo dolls are fashioned out of whatever natural elements available to the region. In New Orleans, Spanish moss and sticks form the basis for many Voodoo dolls. The faces are hand sculpted out of clay with painted details, or made of cloth with sewn facial features, or a natural knot in a piece of wood, for example. Often, the purpose of the Voodoo doll is what dictates how the doll is created and what it is made out of. Fertility dolls may have big breasts and exaggerated genitalia, for example.

Using the principles of sympathetic magic, a Voodoo doll can be made in the image of a particular person to affect that person in some way, be it for the right (good) or left (dark) hand. The person making the doll is believed to infuse that doll with the energy at the time of its creation. If their intent is to deceive and mislead, then the Voodoo doll will carry that energy with it wherever it goes. If the person is angry and quarreling with someone while creating the Voodoo doll, those energies will embody the doll. On the other hand, if a doll is created with positive intention and a loving heart, love and blessings will embody the doll.

If you are purchasing a doll as opposed to making one yourself, be mindful of your intention as the doll and the energy it embodies will be taking up residence in your home. As long as the doll was created with positive, loving energy, you will enjoy having it as a member of your family for years to come. Dolls that are created for darker purposes should be kept in seclusion, and wrapped in white cloth away from the prying eyes and curiosity of others. These dolls should be handled as little as possible. Remember, Voodoo dolls are extremely personal items and flourish when you develop a personal relationship with them.

Heirloom Dolls

Like other kinds of dolls, Voodoo dolls are often passed down from one generation to the next as heirlooms. Heirloom dolls are designed for a specific purpose and serve to keep specific traditions alive within the family. Dolls handed down in this way tend to accumulate generational energy and are often quite powerful. Old-line New Orleans families cherish their heirloom dolls, and it is not uncommon for fertility Voodoo dolls to be given to women in the family who are hoping to conceive. Old-line families are those families in high society who have ancestors that arrived in New Orleans in the 1700s.

Another type of Voodoo doll that was utilized for couples trying to have a second child was made of cloth and cut like conjoined twins, sort of like paper dolls joined at the hands or hips. The twin dolls were given to the first child with the hopes of drawing a brother or sister into the family. These dolls were decorated with charms and baubles for good luck, similar to the old-style ju ju dolls. The dolls would remain attached until the brother or sister arrived, at which time they could be separated. These dolls were unique to New Orleans and are rarely seen anymore.

Devil baby dolls are also hand-crafted family heirlooms, passed down from generation to generation to keep the Devil baby spirit away. The real Devil baby of Bourbon Street has a rich lore in New Orleans with just about as many versions of the legend as there are people telling it. According to one account, in the 1800s, a rich plantation owner who wanted a male heir married a Creole widower. They had six healthy daughters together, and when pregnant for the seventh time, his wife is said to have gone to a Voodoo Hoodoo Queen to ask for help with conceiving a boy child. However, the rich plantation owner was despised by most people, least of all the Voodoo Queen. So, instead of helping, the Voodoo Queen hexed the unborn child, declaring the wife to bear the Devil's son instead of another girl. When the baby was born with red eyes, horns, cloven hooves, claws, and a tail, it was apparent that the Voodoo Queen's black magic worked.

It is said that the ghastly newborn was locked away in the attic loft where he was held captive by his parents. One night during a hurricane, the Devil baby escaped, running wild in the streets, wrecking havoc, eating the neighbor's children, and scaring the life out of anyone who crossed his path. He remained hidden under the buildings of Bourbon Street, where he would emerge to frequent the old Absinthe Bars in New Orleans, attacking the patrons and drinking their absinthe-tainted blood. Many witnessed the demon child wandering the cemeteries for many years. Legend says that the Devil Baby's birthday is on Mardi Gras Day.

Because it was believed that the Devil baby lurked in the shadows of the world, Devil Baby dolls complete with horns and a knotted jute tail were hung in the windows of old cottages to frighten him off. Occasionally, Devil baby dolls would appear on the stoop of unfortunate victims of local workers. Many people claim that their heirloom devil baby dolls are haunted.

Another type of heirloom doll is the Voodoo doll that represents a long-standing hostility between two particular families. These dolls are kept in a secure place by members of subsequent generations, and with each generation, additional protective talismans are added to ensure peace and protection from the arch rival.

Voodoo Moss Dolls

In New Orleans, Voodoo moss dolls can be found all over the French Quarter in a variety of styles, sold as magickal curios infused with the power to heal or hex. These dolls are popular due to their affordability and flexibility. They come in all colors and sometimes carry a gris gris bag (a portable spell) of their own. A person can purchase one of these dolls and use it for whatever purpose is needed. Commonly used purposes are love; power and domination; good luck and prosperity; uncrossing, healing, fertility, protection, and connection with the Divine.

Voodoo moss dolls are typically constructed out of two sticks made into a cross shape and wrapped with Spanish moss. They may also be created out of fabric in the poppet style and stuffed with moss. In New Orleans, you can often find dolls that come with seven pins. The purpose for sticking the pins in the doll corresponds to the color and purpose of the pin. Sticking pins in a Voodoo doll is not meant to cause pain and anguish in another human being; rather, it serves to focus and activate your intention, or for pinning a photograph, personal effect, or name tag to the doll.

Swamp Witch Voodoo Dolls

The wise old woman of the swamp; she has experience of the ancient, the oldest of old, beyond memory, in the roots of the beginning of time. This is the Gran Ibo, most commonly known as the Swamp Witch, so called because the bayou swamp is the place she calls home.

Swamp Witch Voodoo dolls were prevalent up to the 1970s and often came with faces made from dried apples. The Swamp Witch is a goddess/loa of wisdom and patience, and is a healer.

Voodoo Love Dolls

Voodoo Love dolls are arguably the most sought after doll by the general public. These dolls are used for attracting love, improving sex, and getting back an ex. Many times a love Voodoo doll is created as a representation of one of the powerful Voodoo love goddesses, such as Erzulie Freda or Oshun.

Louisiana Broom Dolls

In Louisiana, the broom is a symbol for health and fertility. It also functions to sweep away evil influences from the home. The broom lore actually comes from Hoodoo, or southern African American folklore. Louisiana broom dolls are fashioned out of small brooms as a health, fertility, and protection talismans and are reminiscent of the corn dolly of Europe.

Ju Ju Dolls

Ju Ju dolls are a commonly sought for their good luck and protection properties. The term "ju ju" refers to an object, in this case a doll, that has been blessed and functions to keep evil and negativity away. Sometimes Ju Ju dolls are referred to as guardians because they are used to protect the home from negativity. Other popular ju jus in New Orleans include talismans made of alligator heads and chicken feet. Ju Ju dolls are usually created as poppets, then adorned with colorful yarn, good luck charms, and gris gris bags filled with magickal items to bring positive blessings to their possessor. Ju Ju dolls can be hung above the doorway in your home to keep away evil and negative energy.

Sometimes, ju ju dolls are made in the form of familiars, such as the black cat, one of the most powerful animals in the Voodoo tradition. In the New Orleans Voodoo hoodoo tradition, black cats are considered to be good luck in matters of sports and gambling, particularly with card games and playing the lottery. Black Cat mojo bags are filled with a number of luck-bringing roots and herbs, including John the Conqueror root, and adorned with a small black cat charm on the outside and carried on the person for good luck. Black cat ju ju dolls are adorned with good luck charms and charms that carry a gambling theme, such as tiny dice and playing cards.

Voodoo Devotional Dolls

Devotional dolls are those designed to invoke the power of a specific loa in the life of its possessor. The loas are the deities in the Voodoo pantheon. Artists are often inspired by one of the goddesses, gods, or spirits and create Voodoo dolls according to their understanding and interpretation. Typically, artists incorporate specific characteristics into the doll, such as color, objects, numbers, and clothing that are unique to that deity. Usually these types of dolls are created after consulting with a mambo, priest, or practitioner/artist and are not meant for public display. Rather, they are highly personal and should be kept away from prying eyes and curious hands.

Among the most commonly created loa dolls are Baron Samedi and his wife Manman Brigit, Erzulie Freda, Papa Legba, and Lasiren.

Voodoo Rope Dolls

Another of the traditional style of Voodoo dolls found in New Orleans is made of rope. These Voodoo dolls sometimes came with their own coffins. Rope dolls were often sold as Marie Laveau dolls and had seven pins for working some mojo. Sometimes, you can still find one of these dolls on eBay.

Voodoo Bone Dolls

Making Voodoo dolls out of bones should be no surprise. Bones have played a large role in New Orleans Voodoo Hoodoo as tools of divination, ingredients in mojo bags, and occasionally in the making of Voodoo dolls.

Corn Husk Dolls

Cornhusk dolls are said to have originated with the Northeastern Native Americans more than a thousand years ago. In addition to being children's toys, they were used in sacred healing ceremonies and sometimes as a result of a dream. A doll would be created, and then buried in the earth to allow Mother Earth to disperse the evil present in the dream.

Voodoo dolls made of cornhusks are an old style of doll that used to be prevalent in New Orleans. Whether this style is the result of Native American influences is speculative; however, considering other ways in which Voodoo has been influenced by Native cultures, it is a logical assumption.

Voodoo Wedding Dolls

The Voodoo Doll Wedding Ritual is alive and well in New Orleans. Voodoo dolls are given as cherished wedding gifts to the wedding couple and sometimes, they are also given to every guest at a wedding. The way the old Voodoo hoodoo tradition holds is that before the wedding couple can receive their dolls, the dolls must be passed to each wedding guest where pins are stuck into the dolls while making happy wishes for the couple. According to some believers in the tradition, if you don't get a Voodoo doll as a wedding gift, it is a sure sign of bad luck.

While pins can be stuck anywhere into the dolls, there are some strategic areas that can enhance a specific wish. For example, if you wish money for the couple, then pins are stuck in the groom's pockets. If you wish for a long-lasting love then you would insert pins into the hearts of each doll. For a strong marriage foundation, you would stick pins into the bride's feet. According to Dawn Theard, a contributing writer for the folks at Haunted New Orleans Tours, the most popular location for poking pins on either doll is the groin region. Obviously, the accompanying wish for this pin-stick would be for many happy children.

Once the dolls have circulated throughout the wedding party and the ritual is complete, the dolls are presented to the couple, with the groom getting the bride doll and the bride receiving the groom doll. To ensure a lifetime of love, luck, and fertility, the dolls should be prominently displayed in their new home.

This joyous tradition does not come without its warnings, however. Couples who plan to have a Voodoo Doll Wedding should be certain that there is no one there who may wish ill on their union. One stick by someone directing an evil thought to the couple will ensure the marriage won't survive the first year.

Voodoo Hexing Dolls

The Voodoo hexing doll is a doll created to represent an intended victim and used as a vehicle for placing an obtrusive, dark magic curse upon the person with the intent of causing them harm. An image is created out of wax, the victim's name is carved into the wax, and the doll is then melted over a flame or pricked with pins while an incantation is uttered. A common style of hexing doll in New Orleans was created out of black fabric or a piece of the victim's clothing, and the victim's name was written on a piece of paper and placed into a slit in the back of the doll along with some cayenne pepper or any number of other gris gris, and the doll was then sewn up. The doll would then be bound with cat gut or twine, buried, tortured, or burned according to the perpetrator's will.

Hexes have been used in virtually all cultures as a form of black magic. Hexes and curses are known to be thrown on groups of people as well as families, whereby bad luck befalls a family generation after generation, until the curse is broken.

Hexes are highly discouraged by most practitioners who understand the universal laws of "like begets like", karma, and the Threefold Law. Basically, it is understood that whatever you put out will come back to you three fold, so don't do anything to someone else that you wouldn't want to happen to you amplified times three. Only in specific circumstances is hexing acceptable, and that is in cases of violent criminals, including rapists, and pedophiles. Even in these types of cases, the target is typically bound and rendered harmless.

Voodoo Dolls

Mass produced novelty Voodoo hex dolls are popular items today. You can find one to "hex yo' ex", hex your boss, hex your presidential candidates, hex rival football teams, and you can even send virtual hexes through emails. These "Voodoo" dolls are anything but authentic and certainly reflect the mass appeal of the prevailing stereotypes surrounding Voodoo dolls in contemporary society.

Haitian Vodou Dolls

There is the erroneous belief that Vodou dolls are not a feature of Haitian Vodou, a belief sustained in part by the perpetual copying of an inaccurate passage or two from Wikipedia (the online encyclopedia that anyone can edit) and pasted all over the internet that states as much. This is simply untrue. What is true is that the manner in which they are used is not consistent with the stereotypes that abound. You won't find Haitian followers of the religion sticking pins into dolls in an effort to affect a curse on someone. What you will find is the incorporation of plastic baby dolls, often dismembered, alongside flowers, flaming candles, and various depictions of Jesus and the Virgin Mary adorning altars and featured in sacred Haitian art. Sometimes, china, rubber, and plastic dolls are also used to represent the Vodou spirits.

In a 2003 article in the Miami Herald, the treatment room of a bokor is described as thus:

> Bazile's treatment room, is a dark space at the back of the house. There, you will find burning candles floating in aluminum bowls, and others resting on a makeshift altar next to vodou dolls. The dolls are many. They are mostly black, but there is at least one white one. There is a saintly icon—the black Madonna holding what appears to

be the Christ child. She is Ezili Danto and the child is one of her offspring's. (Charles, 2003).

The heads and torsos of plastic baby dolls are also seen in clear bottles in Haiti, though they are rarely found on altars. How they get inside the bottles is a mystery to me. These bottled baby dolls are apparently used in divination, and are also used as charms to ward off evil.

In addition to plastic baby dolls, one can find cloth Vodou dolls of Haitian origin. Vodou dolls made of cloth are primarily used as mediums to carry messages to the spirit world. These can be found left at the graveyard or the crossroads, sometimes with notes pinned to their bodies. According to Brown (1991), cloth dolls of this type were observed to be used by a Haitian Vodou priestess named Alourdes to influence relationships:

> When a love relationship is desired, Alourdes binds the two dolls face-to-face. When the dissolution of a relationship is desired, the binds them back-to-back. For restive, "hungry" spirits, she prescribes a meal of their favorite foods. To treat a violent marriage, Alourdes makes a charm for the wife by filling a jar with ice ('to cool him down') and molasses ('to make him sweet'). Then she wraps the charm in some article of her husband's clothing and turns the whole thing upside down, a clear signal within the Vodou science of the concrete that a revolutionary change is desired. (Brown, 1991, p. 348).

In addition to Vodou dolls, a variety of spirit-infused artistic objects are used to house or contain spirits and adorn altars, including *Kongo packets*, *govi* (jars), *wanga* (charms), and *po tet* (pots).

Wanga Dolls

Wanga dolls are cloth bundles vaguely resembling human figures and can be used for malevolent or protective purposes through sympathetic magic. Wanga dolls are works of art turned into magickal objects upon consecration and are based on the traditional African wanga pakets. They contain special mixtures of herbs, power objects, and sacred offerings to the Loa.

Harlequin Dolls

Harlequin Voodoo dolls are an old style New Orleans cloth doll that is made in human figure form like a poppet. These dolls were made to be half black and half white to symbolize balance. These dolls provide a focus for meditation when feeling out of balance.

Another interpretation of the harlequin Voodoo doll is that the right side is always black and is used for hexing and cursing. The right side can be red for casting love spells or white for spiritual help. The back of the doll is blue, and is used for attracting good fortune.

Figure 1. Harlequin Voodoo doll stuffed with Spanish moss.

Types of Voodoo Dolls

Photo: 11. Wanga Paket, created by the author.

Types of Voodoo Dolls

Photo: 12. Images on Indian Doctor's grave, Chilkat Alaska, 1895, Winter and Pond.

Voodoo Dolls

Photo: 13. Djab Voodoo doll, created by the author.

Types of Voodoo Dolls

Photo: 14. Swamp Witch Voodoo doll on display at the New Orleans Voodoo Museum.

Photo: 15. Wedding Couple created by the author.

Types of Voodoo Dolls

Photo: 16. Louisiana Fertility Broom Doll created by the author.

Voodoo Dolls

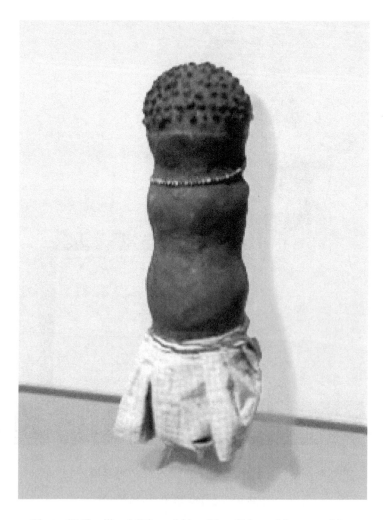

Photo: 17. Fertility doll from Africa, New Orleans Museum of Art.

Types of Voodoo Dolls

Photo: 18. Erzulie Freda, created by the author.

Voodoo Dolls

Photo: 19. Black Cat Ju Ju Doll created by the author.

Types of Voodoo Dolls

Photo: 20. Voodoo Rope Doll created by the author.

Photo: 21. Ju Ju doll created by the author.

Types of Voodoo Dolls

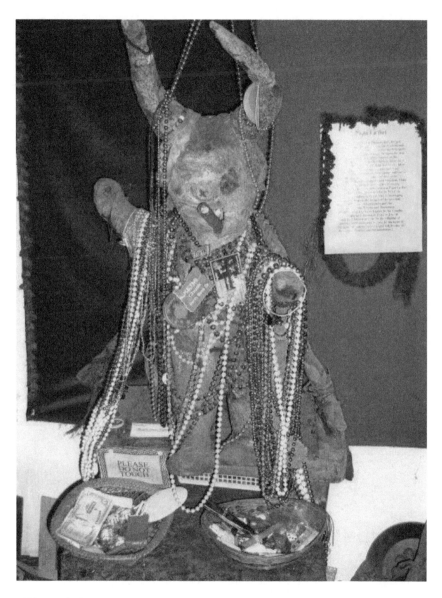

Photo: 22. Papa La Bas at the New Orleans Voodoo Museum, New Orleans, La.

Voodoo Dolls

Photo: 23. Voodoo doll made from chicken bones by the author.

Types of Voodoo Dolls

Photo: 24. A New Orleans Voodoo doll geared towards tourists, from the author's private collection.

Photo: 25. Bound twin mandrake roots by the author.

Types of Voodoo Dolls

Photo: 26. Voodoo Doll – "God to Help You Meet Girls." From the author's private collection.

Voodoo Dolls

Photo: 27. Vintage black Voodoo dolls from the author's private collection.

Types of Voodoo Dolls

Photo: 28. The face of Ogun, Father of Technology. Voodoo doll by the author as seen on National Geographic's Taboo, 2008.

Voodoo Dolls

Photo: 29. Large Voodoo doll with poppet and mandrake doll baby, created by the author.

Types of Voodoo Dolls

Photo: 30. Vintage Voodoo dolls at the New Orleans Voodoo Museum.

Voodoo Dolls

Photo: 31. Corn Husk Voodoo doll.

Types of Voodoo Dolls

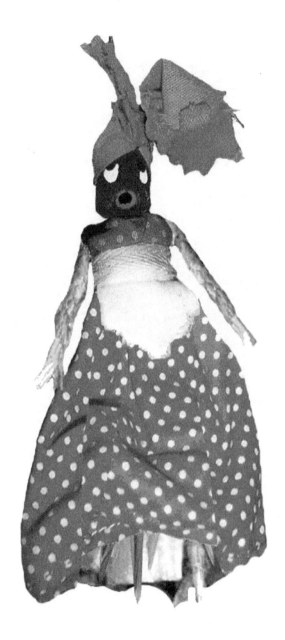

Photo: 32. Black corn dolly.

Photo: 33. Papa Legba Voodoo doll, Guardian of the Crossroads, created by the author.

Types of Voodoo Dolls

Photo: 34. Gran Ibo, the Swamp Witch, created by the author.

Voodoo Dolls

Photo: 35. Very old Voodoo doll of unknown origin. From the author's private collection.

Types of Voodoo Dolls

Photo: 36. Vintage Voodoo doll from Marie Laveau's House of Voodoo, New Orleans, La. The label states the doll is for "intuition." From the author's private collection.

Voodoo Dolls

Photo: 37. Plastic Voodoo doll baby from Martinique, used as a cork. From the author's private collection.

Types of Voodoo Dolls

Photo: 38. Haitian spirit bottle with Voodoo doll baby.

Voodoo Dolls

Photo: 39. Here is a novel Voodoo hexing doll made in the likeness of Ted Thompson, general manager for the Green Bay Packers. He is called "Voodoo Ted", and comes with his own cheesehead hat, rope, and pins. Designed for BluBanana by the author.

Types of Voodoo Dolls

Photo: 40. Dachu Voodoo doll souvenir. From the author's private collection.

Voodoo Dolls

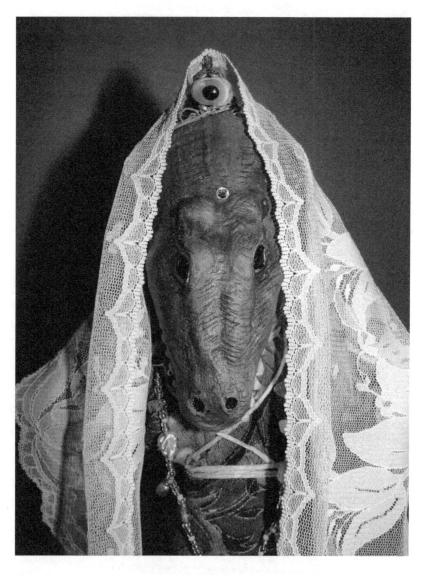

Photo: 41. Swamp Granny hoodoo gator Voodoo doll created by the author. Evil eye bead by Bountiful Bonita.

CHAPTER 4:
How to Make a Voodoo Doll

Making Voodoo dolls can be a lot of fun. It is an activity that elicits laughter and has the potential to facilitate excellent therapeutic conversation among family and friends. Invariably, the stereotypical reasons as to why people make Voodoo dolls comes up, and you have an opportunity to discuss who pissed you off, hurt you, and who deserves a good hexing. What a great forum for a self-help group!

Now, I am the first to admit that there are people in this world who deserve as much bad luck as is humanly and spiritually possible. Child molesters, rapists, sadistic and cruel parents, partners, and world leaders, those involved in the trafficking of women and children for prostitution, my ex-husband...I could go on and on. However, you are strongly encouraged to examine your motives for creating a voodoo doll and to consider the law of three and/or karmic law before proceeding. The law of three essentially states that whatever you will upon someone else will come back to you and yours threefold. Karmic law states that whatever you do will come back to you, and if you believe in reincarnation, you will return as a lower form, putting off reaching ultimate bliss for a long, long time. When you engage in vengeful

Voodoo Dolls

practices, it is spiritually toxic to you, your family, and the universe. There are other, more constructive ways to make an impact that won't subject you or those close to you to the dark forces of the collective shadow of humanity. Few are prepared to deal with such energy. Therefore, be forewarned: these instructions are not in any way intended to encourage the use of Voodoo dolls in a negative fashion, or in any way to cause harm to fall upon anyone. To do so subjects you to karmic forces of your own making, and I assume no responsibility for any illness, unfortunate events, depression, confusion, bad luck, or death that may occur as a result of any activity associated with the making or use of your Voodoo doll.

Today, as in the past, Voodoo dolls are fashioned out of whatever natural elements available to the region. In New Orleans, Spanish moss and sticks form the basis for many Voodoo dolls. The faces are hand sculpted out of clay with painted details, or made of cloth with sewn facial features, or a natural knot in a piece of wood, for example. Often, the purpose of the Voodoo doll is what dictates how the doll is created and what it is made out of. Fertility dolls may have big breasts and exaggerated genitalia, for example. Using the principles of sympathetic magic, a Voodoo doll can be made in the image of a particular person to affect that person in some way, be it for the right (good) or left (dark) hand. The person making the doll is believed to infuse that doll with the energy at the time of its creation. If their intent is to deceive and mislead, then the Voodoo doll will carry that energy with it into your home. If the person is angry and quarreling with someone while creating the Voodoo doll, those energies will embody the doll. On the other hand, if the person creates the doll with positive intention and a loving heart, you will be blessed this way upon receiving the doll.

How to Make a Voodoo Doll

One of the first things to consider before beginning this activity is the type of Voodoo doll you want to make. As you can see from reading the previous chapters, there are countless types of spirits and purposes to inspire the creative process. Here, I will present instructions for making an all-purpose New Orleans-style Voodoo moss doll. In the following chapters, I will provide instructions fro making a Voodoo poppet and a paper Voodoo doll. Keep in mind, however, that there are as many ways of making Voodoo dolls as are people making them! Nonetheless, here are a few basic guidelines to get you started.

Materials

To make an all-purpose Voodoo doll, you will need the following items:

2 strong sticks

Spanish moss

Scrap fabric cut in 2 inch strips, 2 to 3 feet long (color of your choice)

Yarn that complements or contrasts fabric

String, hemp cord, or waxed thread

2 buttons to use as eyes

Needle and thread in a color to match or contrast your fabric

Tacky glue

7 pins with heads in the following colors: red, blue, green, purple, yellow, black, white

Voodoo Dolls

Directions

1. Gather your materials. Make a cross shape with your two sticks. Tie them together with your string. Hemp cord or waxed thread is better than regular string as they tend to be stronger.

Photo: 42. A cross made from two sticks forms the foundation of the Voodoo moss doll.

2. Take the Spanish moss and wrap it around the sticks, starting at the middle for reinforcement, and going up around the head, down to one arm, back across to the other arm, back to the middle, and down to the bottom. If possible, use moss that is connected together in a big enough piece to cover the sticks without breaking it apart. The idea is to wrap the doll in one continuous motion. If you break the moss apart and have to use more than one continuous piece, that is okay. However, you may have to wrap string around the moss to keep it from falling off. If you wrap tight enough, you shouldn't have to use string over the moss.

How to Make a Voodoo Doll

Photo: 43. Wrap the cross with moss.

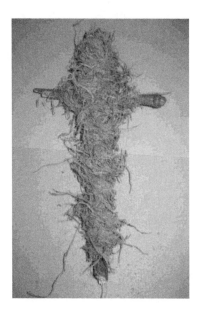

Photo: 44. Cross with full moss

3. Take your fabric strips and wrap around the moss. Make sure to leave some of the moss showing, such as on the head (for hair), at the ends of the arms, and at the bottom. Secure with tacky glue. You may want to reinforce with a couple of stitches with your needle and thread.

Photo: 45. Basic Voodoo Moss Doll

4. Make a face. Take your beads and attach them with the needle and thread for eyes, or glue 2 black eyed peas to the face for eyes. Add a button, bead, whatever you wish for the mouth.

How to Make a Voodoo Doll

Photo: 46. Voodoo doll face with black eyed peas for eyes.

5. Dress your Voodoo doll. This step is entirely optional. However, I always add details like clothes to my dolls because they begin to speak to me and tell me what they want to wear, whether they are male, female, gay, lesbian, or androgynous, and what types of items they want to carry, such as a mojo pouch or gris gris bag. Sometimes

> they are made to look like a person you know, in which case you should have some hair or a piece of clothing or other personal item that belongs to that person in order to charge the doll with that person's energy. In that case, attach the personal item to the doll, or tuck it inside the doll.

Take some yarn or contrasting material and wrap it where you want it for accent. You can make a belt or use it for hair, for example, or make some clothing. Stick some feathers into the moss on the head.

6. Add the seven pins by sticking them into the doll in the chest area.

VIOLA! You have created an all-purpose Voodoo doll!

How to Make a Voodoo Doll

Photo: 47. Voodoo moss dolls.

CHAPTER 5: How to Make a Voodoo Poppet

There are a multitude of ways to make a Voodoo poppet. You can literally make them out of any material you want; you are limited only by your imagination and intention. For example, a poppet doll can be made out of muslin or felt, or a beautiful fabric that you love and makes you feel good. Use the color guidelines below to make your poppet suit a particular purpose. Stitch the dolls up the sides leaving a space at the head open for stuffing. Use batting, herbs, or moss to stuff your Voodoo poppet, include a black-eyed pea for good luck, stitch up the head, and viola! You have your very own handmade Voodoo poppet! Detailed instructions follow.

Color Symbolism for Poppets

Yellow –success, understanding, persuasion, attraction, confidence, charm
White – peace, purity, protection, positivity, healing, health, stop gossip, uncrossing, truth, sincerity
Red – power, domination, passion, love, good health, strength, vigor

Purple – spirituality, spiritual healing, psychic ability and manifestation, psychic healing, power, wisdom, Spirit contact, effective against black magic, demonic possession, can be used to throw up a cloak of Spiritual protection, ambition, business progress

Green – money, wealth, prosperity, nature, material gain, fertility, abundance, good fortune, cooperation, generosity, good health, renewal

Blue – love, commanding, color to honor Marie Laveau

Indigo – sacred color, protection against evil

Pink - affection, generosity, selflessness, domestic love, togetherness, gentleness, good luck, spiritual fulfillment, happiness, friendship, morality

Black – hexing, reversing, transformation, getting rid of bad habits, sadness, evil, discord, loss, confusion

Brown – confusing an enemy, hesitation, uncertainty, doubt

Grey - neutrality, stalemate, cancellation

Orange – success, fortunate dreams, encouragement, adaptation, concentration

Poppet Patterns

Following are several patterns for Voodoo doll poppets. Feel free to copy and print them out to make your own voodoo poppet dolls!

Voodoo Dolls

Basic Poppet Pattern #1

Figure 2. Poppet Pattern #1

Basic Poppet Pattern #2

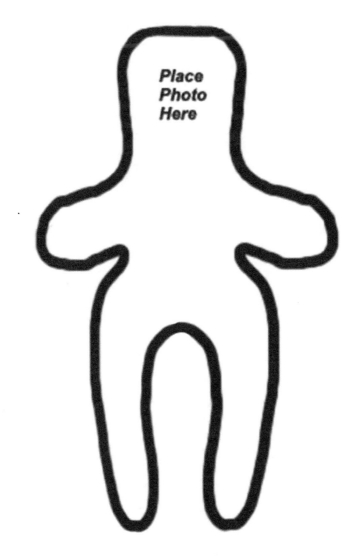

Figure 3. Poppet pattern #2

Poppet Pattern #3: Mermaid

This pattern is ideal for making La Sirene, or Yemaya, or your basic love poppets.

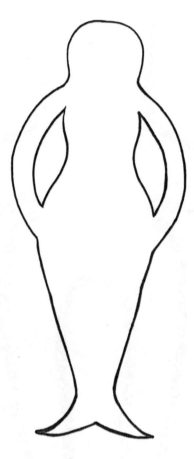

Figure 4. Poppet pattern #3

Poppet Pattern #4: Mermaid

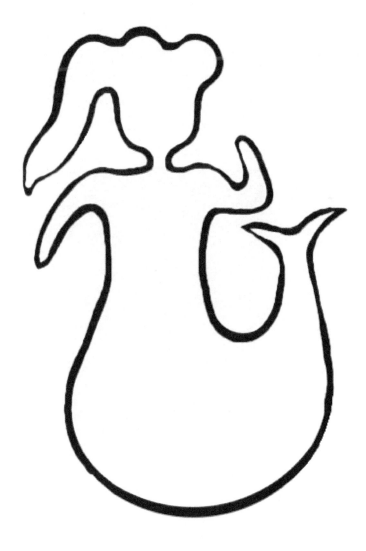

Figure 5. Poppet pattern #4

Directions for Basic Stitches

In order to make your Voodoo poppet, you will need to know how to make a basic blanket stitch or running stitch. The blanket stitch is traditionally used to edge blankets, afghans, and raw seams to keep them from raveling. In addition to being functional, it is also decorative and lends itself well to Voodoo doll making when prominent stitching is often desired. I have provided instructions for each of these stitches below.

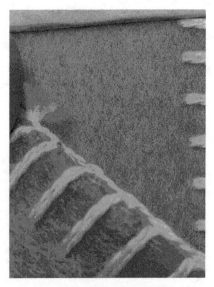

Photo: 48. Blanket stitch

Blanket Stitch

To make the blanket stitch, bring the needle out at point A (outer edge). Working from LEFT to RIGHT, insert at point B (adjusting the amount of spacing to your liking), then with thread below the needle, come out at point C directly below. Continue in this manner, noting that point C now becomes point A for the following stitch. When using this stitch in embroidery or other sewing projects, you would want to be sure to keep the spacing even between stitches. However, when making Voodoo dolls, that is not so important. In fact, uneven stitching lends itself to the primitive nature of conjure crafting (see figure 5).

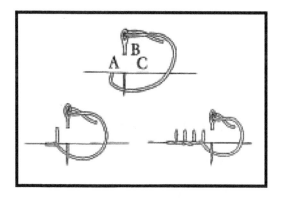

Figure 6. Blanket stitch

Running Stitch

The running stitch is another good stitch to use for making Voodoo poppets. It is easier to do than the blanket stitch, so if you find the blanket stitch too difficult, try this one (see figure 6).

The running stitch or straight stitch is the basic stitch in hand-sewing and embroidery, and is the one upon which all other forms of sewing are based. To make a running stitch, pass the needle in and out of the fabric, making the surface stitches of equal length. The stitches on the underside should also be of equal length, but half the size or less than the upper stitches.

Voodoo Dolls

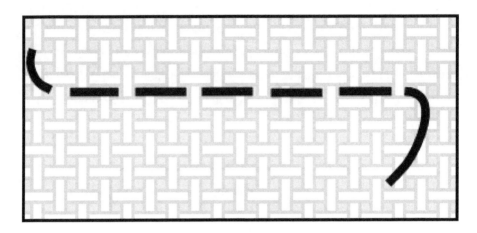

Figure 7. Running Stitch

How to Sew a Voodoo Poppet

Now that you have your patterns and stitches, you can begin assembling your Voodoo poppet doll. These instructions are for how to make a Voodoo poppet out of cloth or leather. For this doll you will need:

Poppet pattern (see previous section for sample patterns or draw your own)
Scissors
Card stock
Black nylon thread or waxed beading thread
Hemp cord
Leather needle
Thin leather
Straight pins
Spanish moss
2-5 buttons
Patience & creativity

How to Make a Poppet

Directions

1. Pick out a pattern from the previous section or draw your own and cut it out on card stock.

Photo: 49. Basic poppet pattern.

2. Place your pattern on a piece of fabric or leather.

Photo: 50. Pattern is placed on top of leather.

Voodoo Dolls

3. Pin the pattern to the leather with your straight pins.

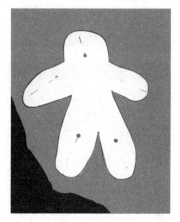

Photo: 51. Pattern is pinned to leather to keep from sliding around.

4. Cut out the pattern, leaving about 1/4 inch seam allowance. Repeat step four, so you have two sides.

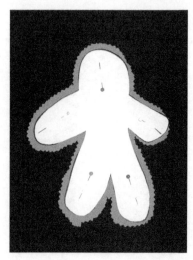

Photo: 52. This pattern was cut out using pinking shears.

How to Make a Poppet

5. Unpin the paper patterns. Cut the leather down the middle of each side (optional).

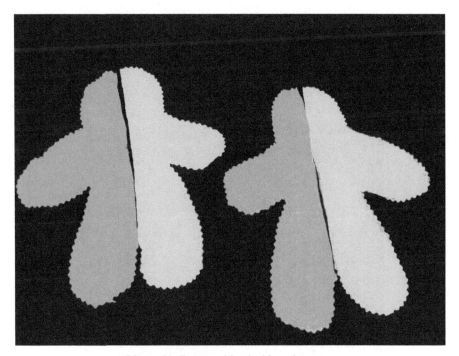

Photo: 53. Front and back sides of poppet.

Artist hint: leather has two different looks. One side is smooth and the other side is rougher. Also, one side is typically lighter than the other. I decided to make one half dark and the other half light. This is purely aesthetic and not necessary, but I think it makes him look cool. It is also a sort of take on the traditional New Orleans harlequin dolls that are made using half black and half white material.

Voodoo Dolls

6. Place the patterns together and sew around the entire edge of the voodoo doll using a blanket stitch or running stitch. On one side of the doll sew all the way up the middle.

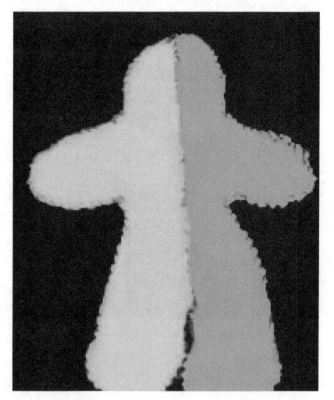

Photo: 54. The two sides are sewn together.

7. On the other side, starting from the head, sew halfway down. From the bottom, sew halfway up. You should have an opening on one side of the doll where you will put the stuffing. You can leave the feet and arms open if you want. I sewed the hands on mine, and left the feet open.

How to Make a Poppet

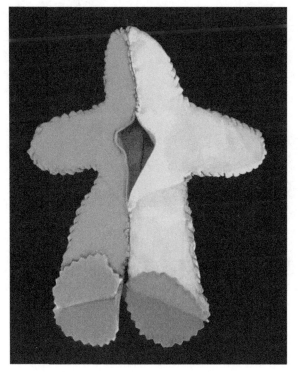

Photo: 55. A small opening is left on one side of the poppet for stuffing.

8. Take the Spanish moss and stuff your voodoo doll with it.

Voodoo Dolls

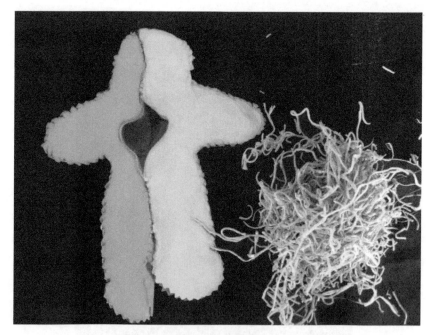

Photo: 56. Poppet and Spanish moss.

If you want, you can turn the pattern inside out first. This is entirely optional and depends on how you want him to look. I turned mine inside out. When you are done stuffing, it should look like this:

How to Make a Poppet

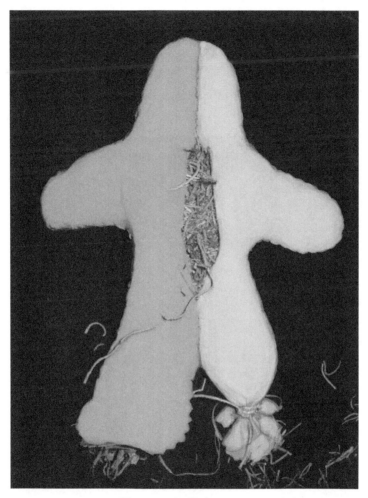

Photo: 57. Stuffed poppet.

Mojo magick hint: if you intend to use this voodoo doll ritualistically, now is the time to place other herbs, curios, and personal items inside to make him magickal and powerful. Because I want mine to bring business success to his

Voodoo Dolls

ultimate possessor, I placed some sage inside and infused it with sage essential oil, about 15 drops. I also placed a piece of fool's gold and a silver dime inside and dressed with magnetic sand for its drawing properties. He smells awesome!

9. Sew the opening closed. Tie the feet closed with the hemp cord. If you left the hands open, now is the time to tie the hands closed.

Photo: 58. Stuffed poppet with buttons sewn on for eyes.

Now you have your basic voodoo poppet doll!

More Ways to Make Poppets

Here are some more ways you can make poppets – from wax to paper to wood and more.

Wax Poppets

To make a wax poppet, coat you hands with a few drops of essential oil, and mold a shape out of softened wax and adorn it with stones, beads, or draw names or symbols into the form. You can add hair or nail clippings or some other personal effect of the person it represents.

Root Poppets

Root poppets can be made out of naturally shaped roots that look like figures, or they can be carved out of root vegetables like potatoes. In the past, they have been made out of mandrake roots or ginseng which can look amazingly human in form.

Mandrake poppets are also called fetishes. Superstitious people were so afraid of the appearance of mandrake roots that they would draw a circle around it or tie a dog to the plant to protect themselves when the root was pulled from the ground. It was believed that the mandrake could kill a person from the screams so powerful. The root was worn around the neck.

Men and lesbian women should carry with them the feminine, White Mandrake (Mandragora officinarum var. vernalis), or the substitute, White Bryony (Bryonia dioica).

Women and homosexual men should carry with them the masculine, Black Mandrake (Mandragora officinarum var. autumnalis) or the substitute, Black Bryony (Tamus communis).

Clay Poppets

Clay poppets are molded out of any number of types of clay. In New Orleans, a traditional type of Voodoo doll involves constructing the doll out of the clay from crawfish holes. Create a hollow space in the clay to place personal effects of the spell recipient, or fill with special herbs or drawn symbols and then seal. Paint or adorn the clay accordingly.

Wood Poppets

Wood poppets can be made in a number of ways. One way is to simply nail a couple of pieces of scrap wood together. Another way is to carve a figure form out of soft wood. Glue hair to the head or yarn representing hair, and paint the wood with acrylic paint. You can paint symbols, names or paint clothes, or a face. You are limited only by your imagination.

Paper Poppets

Paper Voodoo poppets are the easiest of all of the dolls to make. They are quick, yet effective. The next chapter provides detailed instructions for making your own paper Voodoo dolls. Make one, and then use it in spells that call for Voodoo dolls.

CHAPTER 6:
How to Make a Paper Voodoo Doll

There are a multitude of ways to make a paper Voodoo doll. Like making a cloth Voodoo poppet, you can literally make them out of any kind of paper material you want; you are limited only by your imagination and intention. For example, a poppet doll can be made out of construction paper, wallpaper, or a beautiful scrapbook paper that you love and makes you feel good. Or they can simply be made out of paper. Use the color guidelines in the previous chapter to make your poppet suit a particular purpose. Then, use the following symbols to further personalize your paper Voodoo doll.

Symbols for Drawing or Pasting on Paper Voodoo Dolls

Below are some suggested symbols for use on your paper Voodoo dolls. Draw them or photocopy them and cut them out, then paste them to you Voodoo doll. You are not limited to the designs here; these are simply suggestions to get you started.

Figure 8. Symbols for Use with Paper Voodoo Dolls

Good luck & success	Positive Healing	Power	Spirituality, psychic ability	Money, wealth, prosperity	Love

Paper Voodoo Doll Patterns

To make a paper poppet, draw a figure on a piece of card stock or parchment paper. You can either cut it out or leave the paper intact. On the paper doll, draw symbols and write the name of the intended recipient of the spell. You can affix a photo onto the face if you have one. Then use it in spells that call for Voodoo dolls.

Following are several patterns for Voodoo doll poppets, including two mandrake patterns to be used in love spells. Feel free to copy and print them out to make your own voodoo poppet dolls! Use the color and symbol guidelines above for personalizing your paper Voodoo poppet doll.

Paper Voodoo Doll Pattern #1

9. Paper Voodoo doll pattern

Mandrake Poppet Doll Pattern #2: Female

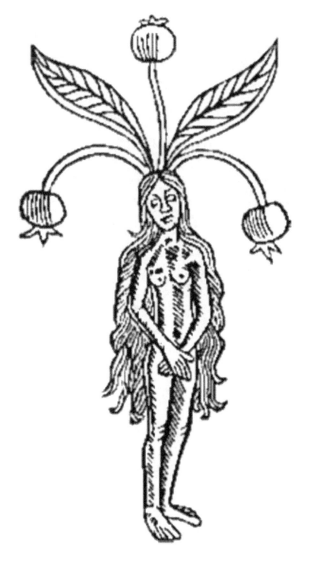

10. Female mandrake

Mandrake Poppet Doll Pattern #3: Male

11. Male mandrake

Paper Voodoo Doll Pattern #4: Mermaid

12. Mermaid (La Sirene)

CHAPTER 7:
How to Prepare your Voodoo Doll for Ritual Use

The process for making a Voodoo doll to use in ritual and meditation involves *charging* it. Charging is an essential part of any type of magick system. This is a relatively simple process, assuming you have the ability to focus and direct your energy towards a target object. You can charge any kind of object, from sigils and talismans, to dolls and mojo bags.

Classic ritual charging requires directing your energy towards something and feeding it with your energy. When you draw a sigil or create a talisman, all you have to do is place your hand over the drawing and focus your intention. However, to charge a Voodoo doll, you must complete at least three, if not four steps, depending on the nature of the work. The four steps are: (a) clearing, (b) creation, and (c) consecration, and (d) baptism. Note that you will not have to baptize your doll unless you want to name it. I will describe these steps in further detail in the following sections.

Clearing

Clearing an object is the process by which you neutralize or remove the energy that exists in it. In essence, clearing gives you a clean slate from which to perform your ritual work. This is a necessary step to perform prior to creating your doll and ultimately consecrating or baptizing it.

There are a number of items that are needed to create a Voodoo doll. Aside from the natural items obtained from Mother Earth, there may be beads, buttons, fabric, thread, paint, glue, feathers, string, etc. Think about the number of hands each of these items has been through in the process of their own creation. Brand new items will be relatively clear, but will still have residual energy from the people and/or machines that created them. If you are using items given to you by someone else, items that you bought, or items won in an auction, there will be energy attached to the items that are not aligned with your specific purpose. On the other hand, if you are using items given to you by a mentor or teacher, or items that have been blessed by a priestess, then you may want to retain that energy and supplement it with your own.

There are many ways to clear an object. For example, you can place your hand over the object and direct your energy through it, you can wash the item with saltwater, you can sprinkle the item with salt, you can smudge it with purifying incense such as sandalwood or sage, you can place it in the sunlight or moonlight, or you can bury it in the earth and allow Mother earth to transform the energy. It doesn't matter which of these methods you choose - just pick one and do it!

Creation

Creating a Voodoo doll for use in ritual work involves more than merely slapping together a couple of sticks, and wrapping them with moss and cloth. It is a creative process that involves your will and imagination, changing your mind state, and directing your energy.

The entire act of creating a Voodoo doll is part of the charging process. For some, the process of creating a Voodoo doll is a conjuring process. I cannot emphasize this enough. This is why it is extremely important to be mindful of your intent and exercise self discipline with regards to your behavior during this process, including your thoughts and the words that you speak. You must prepare to mesmerize. If you are unable or unwilling to do this, then you have no business working any kind of magick, much less creating a Voodoo doll.

The first thing you should do is anoint yourself with some holy oil or Seven African Powers oil and say a short prayer or meditation asking the Universe or Higher Power to work with you in the process and help you to accomplish your goals. Try to achieve a trance like state that is in complete harmony with the change you desire to create (this is mesmerizing). You will be able to feel it when you have achieved this. You may feel a little dreamy and calm, and you may feel like you have your feet in two worlds; one in the world of Spirit, and the other in the world of the mundane. This simple act helps to put your mind, heart, and spirit in the right place for creating your doll.

While it is not completely necessary, you can be mindful of the phase of the moon when creating your Voodoo doll. For example, it is good to create your doll when the moon is waxing (growing larger) for drawing rituals.

Drawing spells are spells that involve bringing something to you, such as love, luck, or money. It is good to create your doll when the moon is waning (growing smaller) for banishing spells, or spells of a negative nature like hexing.

Next, it is essential that you are mindful of your intent for creating the doll. If you are creating a doll to bring you luck in financial matters for example, you will want to focus all of your thoughts and energy on having money, paying off your debts, or whatever may be the case. You should visualize success in whatever your intent is, as this is part of the manifesting process.

Finally, be mindful of the words you speak. Words are energy, and whatever tone and subject you project will be projected right into your doll. So it is wise not to yell, curse, gossip, or otherwise speak negatively while creating your doll. If you do so you will be capturing that energy into the doll and your doll will be the essence of the feelings and words used during its creation.

Consecration

The final order of business for ritually charging a Voodoo doll is to consecrate the doll. The act of consecration involves opening up to and tapping into the Universal Divine force from which all possibilities, solutions, and miracles emanate. To consecrate an object for ritual use is to connect to this Universal Divine force and to declare sacred or appropriate for sacred use the object at hand.

Consecrating an object removes any negativity that may be attached to the object and purifies it. It removes the vibrational energies of anyone who has handled the object other than you. This is the foundation of any effective magick or ceremonial work.

To consecrate your Voodoo doll, you will consecrate the items you use to create the Voodoo doll, as well as the Voodoo doll itself once it is completed. To do so is a simple process. You will need your materials (prior to creation), your Voodoo doll (once it is completed), a white candle, and some sage, cedar, or sandalwood incense, and something to burn the herbs or incense in, such as a shell or fireproof dish. So, you will perform a consecration twice: once with the materials used to create the doll, and once after the doll is created. To perform the consecration, follow the steps outlined below.

Step One

Light a white candle. White is the color for purity. Light the herbs or incense.

Step Two

Pass the object through the smoke. This is referred to as "smudging". Repeat the following:

"I hereby consecrate this (name the item) with the powers of earth, water, fire, air, and spirit. That it shall be used only for good, according to my will and Divine law. May it serve me well in this world, between worlds, and in all worlds. So Mote It Be."

Repeat Step Two 6 more times, for a total of seven times. Your objects will now be ready for ritual use. You may personalize what you say; the above is only meant as a guideline. There is no one right way to consecrate an object, place, or person in terms of the words spoken.

Once consecrated, you should not allow others to handle the items or the doll. After consecrating your doll, place it on an altar, or wrap it up safely in a white bag or cloth and put in a safe place where it will not be disturbed.

Baptism

If you have created a doll or poppet to represent another person, you will need to baptize the doll in the name of your target. Naming the doll is the first step to awakening it, or making it come to life. To perform a Voodoo doll baptism, you will need some holy water or holy anointing oil and the doll.

How to Baptize a Voodoo Doll

Light a white candle. Repeat the following words, replacing (Name) with the name of your doll, and using the name of your personal Higher Power as appropriate.

"I baptize thee (Name), in the name of the Father, Son and Holy Ghost (you may substitute your personal Higher Power here). In life, this is now that who I wish you to be. All that is asked of you happens now as I so do command."

"As day goes by and time is infinite, I alone now control the deepest desires, dreams, and actions of (Name of doll or person whom the doll represents). Your life is now as joyful servant to me and my family, you are mine to control, for my purpose alone."

If the doll is to function as an heirloom doll, add the following:

"I welcome (Name) to my home, to my family, and to generations to come. May (Name) only bring pleasure, protection, and profit to me, my family, and my descendents, forever and always, it is now governed, shaped, and controlled only by me. "

End baptism ritual by saying:

"With the highest blessings of our most High Lord. So mote it be."

Sprinkle a little Holy water on the doll, and the baptism is complete.

If this will be an heirloom doll, this baptism ritual should be passed down to the next generation where the keeper of the doll should repeat the ritual at the time they take possession of the doll.

A Word of Warning

Do not baptize or name your doll unless you intend to use it. There are numerous stories of people having done exactly that, only to be plagued by ill fortune assumed to be associated with the doll.

CHAPTER 8:
Voodoo Doll Magick

What is your desire? Ancient spells for luck, love, or fortune? Placing a curse on your enemy? Bringing back a lost love? Hexing your foe? Oh, the possibilities!

So far, we have seen the many ways in which Voodoo dolls have been used throughout history and across cultures. One thing that these cultures understood was the concept of image magick, and how to employ dolls in conjunction with image magick for protection, revenge, and love. So, the following section is a crash course on image magick to help those readers who are not familiar with such concepts make better sense of how Voodoo dolls are used most effectively.

Principals of Image Magick

In order to understand how Voodoo dolls work, or how people work Voodoo dolls, it is necessary to understand the basic principles of image magick. *Magick* is a conceptual system that emphasizes the human ability to manipulate and predict the natural world (including events, objects, people, and physical phenomena) through mystical, paranormal or supernatural means. Magick is employed in a variety of ways, such as the use of ritual symbols, magick words, wands and other ritual tools, herbs, dance, and trance. One goal of these activities is to evoke or invoke spirits to assist with the matter at hand. Some of the principles of magick include:

1. Manipulation of natural forces that are currently undetectable by science;
2. Manipulation of symbols, seals, and sigils to influence reality and summon spirits;
3. Intervention of spirits;
4. Manipulation of energy to influence people and events, or to heal;
5. Concentration and meditation;
6. Visualization; you must have very clear ideas about what it is that you want to do;
7. Cocreation, or the belief in aligning oneself with universal forces to manifest in tandem with the universe the change you seek;
8. The Law of Three, which means that whatever you do to someone else will come back to you threefold;
9. The law of karma or cause and effect;
10. The need to be sensitive to what is occurring on all dimensions of reality, such as the physical, astral, mental, and spiritual planes;
11. Principles of image magic, such as *like attracts like* or the law of similarity, and the law of contagion.

There are many more principles of magick, but it is the latter example of image magick that is most applicable to Voodoo dolls in magick and ritual. *Image magick* is a type of magick based on the principles of *like attracts like* or *correspondence*. This type of magick involves using effigies or dolls to affect the environments and situations of people or people themselves. Correspondence is based on the idea that one can influence something based on its relationship to another thing.

There are two types of image magic: sympathetic magic and contagious magic. According to Frazer (1922):

> If we analyze the principles of thought on which magic is based, they will probably be found to resolve themselves into two: first, that like produces like, or that an effect resembles its cause; and, second, that things which have once been in contact with each other continue to act on each other at a distance after the physical contact has been severed. The former principle may be called the Law of Similarity, the latter the Law of Contact or Contagion. From the first of these principles, namely the Law of Similarity, the magician infers that he can produce any effect he desires merely by imitating it: from the second he infers that whatever he does to a material object will affect equally the person with whom the object was once in contact, whether it formed part of his body or not. (Frazer, 1922).

Perhaps the most familiar application of image magick is the attempt to injure or destroy and enemy by injuring or destroying and image of them. There are countless examples across cultures and throughout history of the use of dolls in image magick. For example, Peruvian Indians would mold a human figure from fat mixed with grain to imitate the persons whom they feared or did not like. They would then burn the little doll on the road where the intended victim would cross. This was referred to as *burning his soul* (Frazer, 1922). In hoodoo, this type of magick is called *foot track magick* or *laying tricks*. Foot track magick involves throwing powders and such in the path of a target, who will suffer from abnormal maladies and a streak of bad luck once they have walked on it. Laying tricks is another reference to the throwing of special herbs, powders and other ingredients in a place where the intended target will touch it, usually by walking on it. It also refers to concealing or disposing of magickal objects by strategically placing the ingredients in certain places in order to *fix the trick*; in essence, to seal the deal, as it were. For example, if one wants to keep their partner faithful, they could take a pair of their lover's dirty underwear, tie it in a knot, and bury it in their backyard (Alvarado, 2008).

Another example of image magick is a Malay charm. One would fashion a corpse doll representing the enemy out of beeswax and poke the eye of the doll to blind the enemy, pierce the stomach to make him or her sick, stab the doll in the head to give the enemy a headache, and pierce the chest to give him or her a heart attack. To kill the enemy, one would carry out a sort of mock funeral, including covering the doll in a shroud and praying over the corpse as if it were a real dead person. The doll would then be buried in the middle of the path where the victim was sure to cross. To ensure absolution, one would transfer the guilt of the murder onto the archangel Gabriel by uttering the following words while burying the doll: *"It is not I who am burying him, It is Gabriel who is burying him"* (Frazer, 1922).

How to Use a Voodoo Doll

Thanks to Hollywood and general ignorance, the most popular misconception about Voodoo dolls is that they are made to exact revenge against enemies. Just type in Voodoo doll in any search engine and you are guaranteed to come up with countless sites that promise to sell you a Voodoo doll with instructions for hexing someone, casting a revenge spell, or placing a curse on your enemy. These dolls come complete with pins for inflicting illness or harm upon someone and complete justification for doing so. One site I found stated "Witchcraft spells, hexes and voodoo curses are meant to enhance your life and assist you in many situations & help", and equated Voodoo with the "dark side of this magical spiritual world" and working with Voodoo dolls as "the Black Arts". The justification used for hexing someone is that it is okay if someone has hurt you through no fault of your own, and that you are not wishing more harm upon that person than was inflicted upon you. It is assumed that you are protected from any type of karmic backlash because this "fair use" of the Voodoo doll is not contrary to any Universal laws.

There are several things wrong with this type of thinking and advertising. First of all, it is inaccurate on so many levels. For example, most practitioners of magick and Voodoo today do not use pins in Voodoo dolls - at least not for exacting revenge. When pins are used, they are used to direct or activate healing energy into a particular area of the doll. Secondly, Voodoo is not a form of the Black Arts. Voodoo is a legitimate religion that largely originated in Africa and melded with elements of European folk magic and Indigenous herbology and beliefs to become what it is today. Most aspects of Voodoo are positive, concerned with healing, and guides its followers in matters of daily living, as most religions do. Voodoo was brought to the Americas through slavery and the colonization process. Its condemnation and inaccurate representation is as much the result of racism as slavery is.

Next, any tool used for magickal purposes can be charged to possess positive or negative vibrations through ceremony or meditation periodically in association with phases of the moon. In this way, the tool becomes alive and something to be respected. If misused, you will feel the karmic effects through conflicts, accidents, depression, or bad luck for example. This is why it is extremely important to exercise caution when using your Voodoo doll.

Voodoo Dolls

Voodoo dolls can be used for dark purposes; however, this is never a good idea. There **IS** karmic backlash associated with using Voodoo dolls with the intent of hurting someone else. That is why all of the reputable practitioners who sell Voodoo dolls indicate their dolls are blessed to carry only positive energy and light with them. You would be wise to follow suit.

Because Voodoo dolls can absorb energies from people who have used them, it is a good idea to never use someone else's Voodoo dolls or any other magickal tool, for that matter. Common sense applies here: you wouldn't use someone else's toothbrush, right? In the same way you shouldn't work with someone else's Voodoo dolls.

Here is a list of the possible ways in which Voodoo dolls can be used (thought not all are recommended):

- Use as a focusing tool in ritual and meditation.
- Use as a therapeutic tool.
- Use in spells of love and attraction.
- Use to inflict harm upon another person (not recommended).
- Use in banishment rituals.
- Use in binding rituals.
- Use to send a powerful psychological message to someone.
- Use as in sympathetic magic where the doll represents a particular person or situation.
- Use in healing rituals.
- Use as a guardian of the home.

I will describe some of these in further detail next.

Use Your Voodoo Doll as a Focusing Tool

By far the most common use of a Voodoo doll is their use as focusing tools. Typically, you appeal to the loa (deity) that your doll represents, light a candle in the appropriate color of the loa, and make offerings to the loa. For example, to use a Papa Legba Voodoo doll as a focusing tool you would light a red or black candle (his favorite colors), and greet him with his ritual greeting, "Odu Legba, Papa Legba, open the door I am waiting. Open the door Papa Legba, I am waiting. On my way back, I will return the favor." You can then tell him your wishes and offer him some of his favorite things in three (his favorite number). Things he likes are candy, corn, rum, and cigars. Don't forget to tell him to close the door when you are finished.

Use Your Voodoo Doll as a Therapeutic Tool

Voodoo dolls can be used therapeutically to express anger or hurt about another person. The intent must be very clear here; using a Voodoo doll therapeutically means processing your feelings about someone or some event in your life. The feelings expressed must be yours and the desired end is a transformation of your hurtful and destructive feelings into wisdom or something constructive. For this exercise, you can do anything you want to the doll as a means of releasing negative emotions and emotions that bind you to the negative event. This can be effectively done in therapy, with a trusted friend or elder, or by yourself if you are emotionally strong enough to handle the feelings that emerge from the exercise.

Use Your Voodoo Doll for Revenge

Okay, so there are people in this world whom we would all love to hex and who deserve a massive cursing...like child rapists and my ex-husband, for example. I am not denying this fact. Is it ever okay to wish excruciating pain and dismemberment on these types of people? Well, yes and no. Most practitioners would agree that in cases of murder, rape, sexual abuse, and child abuse, revenge is appropriate. Even in these cases, it is better to proceed in a manner that renders the other person harmless, instead of inflicting pain.

Can You Really Kill Someone with a Voodoo Doll?

Murder, torture, abuse, maim, dismember...these are some of the words commonly associated with Voodoo dolls in the popular culture. People turn to the extreme to get even, gain control over, torture, and even kill their enemies. But can you really torture a person with A Voodoo doll? First, let's take a candid look at the process of torturing an enemy with a Voodoo doll. Torture by Voodoo doll is:

1. Inflicting severe pain by sticking pins in the groin or other area to force information or confession, get revenge, etc.

2. Any method by which such pain is inflicted, such as binding, burying alive, or cutting and dismembering.

3. Any severe physical or mental pain, agony, and anguish caused by crushing the head of a Voodoo doll that resembles or represents an intended victim.

4. A cause of such pain or agony, such as fire (burning a voodoo doll), knives (stabbing a voodoo doll), scissors (cutting a voodoo doll), or brute force (beating a voodoo doll)

5. Physical abuse of such severity that it results in the ultimate Voodoo death.

Believe it or not, there are people who seriously want to know if you can kill someone with a Voodoo doll...like, for real. I get asked this question on a weekly basis.

Hmm, there *is* the Santa Clara County murder case involving Damon Wells aka Son of the Devil. Apparently, Damon experimented with voodoo and devil worship, and would frequently talk about demons and black magic at home and at high school. He claimed to hear the devil's voice and claimed he could read other peoples thoughts. He made several voodoo dolls which he would use to hurt people, one of which depicted a bully from school. His school mates tended to avoid him, except this bully, an older boy in the 12th grade, who would delight in teasing him.

According to investigative records, years later Damon sought revenge against this particular tormentor. He took the bully's picture from their high school yearbook, created a special voodoo doll, and repeatedly cast spells and called upon the Devil to destroy him. Coincidentally this bully is reported to have stabbed and killed his pregnant wife, finally turning the knife upon himself. He claimed to have been possessed by the devil.

Is this story true? I haven't a clue.

Then, there is the case of the whole population of Taiwan looking to Voodoo dolls to topple their president Chen Shui-bian in 2006. Reportedly, 7000 Shui-bian Voodoo dolls were snatched up in a matter of hours at an anti Shui-bian rally.

I guess Taiwan is not the only country/province/state/region in China (I'm not sure what the politically correct term is at this point so I thought I would cover all of my bases) to resort to Voodoo dolls to topple

Voodoo Dolls

their presidents. I mean, look at the popular George W Voodoo dolls, Osama Bin Laden Voodoo Dolls, Tony Blair, Bill Clinton...the list is endless. Oh, and let's not forget the Saddam Hussein Voodoo doll; I guess that one worked.

For years people have believed they can hurt or kill others with Voodoo dolls. In 2008, for example, the city commissioner of Deltona, Florida found a voodoo doll complete with pins and her face attached to it, next to her mailbox one weekend. Apparently, someone is not too happy with the state of affairs there.

So, can you like, kill someone with a Voodoo doll? For this question, I will let you be the judge.

CHAPTER 9:
The Meaning of the Seven Pins

Symbolism is an inherent characteristic of all magickal systems, mystical practices, and religions. In addition, there is positive and negative in all magickal systems - good and evil, black and white, light and dark, love and revenge, right and left. While Hollywood and the mass media have inaccurately amplified the negative aspects of Hoodoo and Voodoo and thus perpetuated its traumatic origins in this country, Voodoo priests and priestesses work primarily with the right hand (for good). Hoodoo root doctors, as they are called, will often work with both hands. However, all healers must have an intimate knowledge of both sides of the coin, for without knowledge of the dark, it would be impossible to define the light.

Numbers and colors are at the core of Hoodoo and Voodoo symbology. It is hard to definitively say where the importance of the number seven came from. The number seven is integral to many Native American belief systems, representing the seven sacred directions, and it is commonly known that much of Hoodoo and Voodoo came from the indigenous knowledge of the healing plants and herbs in ritual and healing practices. In addition, it is believed that the availability of the Jewish menorah candle holders were widely available and purchased by practitioners and ultimately the use of seven candles, seven colors, and the number seven in general were incorporated into the practice.

If you research the topic at all, you will find discrepancies into the meanings of the seven colors. I am offering one interpretation of the meanings of the seven colored pins found in New Orleans Voodoo. Note that this interpretation is based on right hand Voodoo practice. The seven pins are meant to assist you in focusing your thoughts and energy in meditation and ritual. Use the various colors to help you achieve your goals:

Yellow - success
White – positive, health
Red - power
Purple - spirituality
Green - money
Blue - love
Black - repelling negative energy

Where to Stick It

There are countless ways to use your pins with your Voodoo doll. The simplest way is to take each pin and concentrate on the color symbolism. Meditate upon how you want these things to manifest in your life. For example, with your yellow pin, focus on what success you desire. After you are very clear about this, stick the pin into your doll in the heart or stomach region. This area will support your heart's desire and your gut feelings or intuition. You can also stick your pins into the head for knowledge. Repeat this process for each pin. I recommend burning a candle during this process to strengthen your work. Choose a candle color to match your deepest need. The candle colors are the same as the pin colors in this case. All that is left to do is to wait and trust in your personal power that the Universe will help you make your intentions manifest. Patience is your best attribute now.

Karmically Incorrect Use of the Seven Pins

If you are arrogant enough to believe you are above the law of karma, then feel free to use your pins in the following way. Just remember that the law of three and the Law of Attraction in magick states that you reap what you sow three-fold, so don't say I didn't warn you!

To make your Voodoo doll represent a person, place some of that person's hair or a personal item inside the cloth of the doll to capture part of their soul. Use your black pin into the part of the body that you want the person to experience negativity. For example, a pin in the heart can cause heartbreak or heart problems, the stomach a stomach ache, the back a back ache or relationship problems, etc. With each stick you must focus your intention with the utmost clarity. Then place the doll on the person's doorstep or in their mailbox and watch the person totally freak out. Or bury it away from your home or in the yard or garden of your enemy, but you are really asking for trouble here...Then back up and watch all hell break loose (in YOUR life, that is)!

Please note that I do not advise using your doll in this way. Voodoo is a powerful magickal system and the law of karma will not make an exception for you. Use of your Voodoo doll in any fashion other than with the right hand as I have recommended may result in severe negative consequences. You have been duly warned!

CHAPTER 10:
Spells and Rituals

Voodoo dolls are mysterious figures, evoking feelings of intrigue, dread, curiosity, and adoration. Like their antecedents, the minkisi, bocio, and paket Kongo, Voodoo dolls can be used for directing energy in a number of ways, from paying homage to ancestors, to functioning as objects of devotion, to serving as objects of concentrated power. Voodoo dolls are excellent for use in spell casting, particularly in cases of attracting love, improving your financial situation, and defeating your enemies. Make your own Voodoo dolls and poppets and use some of the following spells to work your mojo.

BANISH, BIND, AND ENEMY BE GONE

The following spells are for getting rid of an enemy or rival, making someone stop bothering you, or rendering a person harmless. For these types of situations, you can appeal to Ogun or Chango, or for women victims of domestic violence, appeal to Erzulie Dantor. These types of spells are best performed under a waning moon.

Spell to Bind Someone Dangerous

This spell is best performed on Saturday (Saturn's Day, to bind a criminal, one who intends to do harm, to bring someone to justice). For this spell you will need:

a poppet made to represent the person in question
a black candle
myrrh incense
red ribbon
personal effect from the person (not necessary, but helpful)

Light a black candle and burn myrrh incense. Sprinkle the poppet with salt water, saying:

> *Blessed be, thou creature made of art.*
> *By art made, by art changed.*
> *Thou art not cloth (or wax, whatever it is made out of)*
> *But flesh and blood.*
> *I name thee _____ (name the person being bound). Thou art s/he, between the worlds, in all the worlds, So be it.*

Hold the poppet and imagine it captured in a silver net, wrapping around the person in question. Tie the poppet up firmly with red ribbon, binding all parts of it that could possibly do harm. Charge the doll by saying:

> *By air and earth,*
> *By water and fire,*
> *So be you bound,*
> *No longer harm me,*
> *Your power gone,*

Voodoo Dolls

As I desire.

Bury the poppet at the time of the waning moon, far from your home, under a heavy rock.

Banishment and Equalizer Spell

This spell asks God to be the mediator between you and your enemy by protecting you and punishing the person who hurt you.

This spell can be used as a means to settle the score with an enemy, by causing them to be ostracized, resulting in mental anguish, and eventually going away. Since you are asking God to intervene for you, you are not subject to any ill effects or bad karma.

Write the name of your target on the parchment paper and anoint with Black Arts oil. Tuck the paper into the Voodoo doll. Recite Psalm 55 nine times over the doll, and stick one pin through the parchment paper and into the doll. Wrap the doll in a black cloth and hide in a dark place, careful to choose a place where no one can find it and handle it.

Each day for eight more days (for a total of nine days), take out the doll and recite Psalm 55 nine times over it and stick a pin through the parchment paper and into the doll. Wrap the doll in a black cloth and hide away in a dark place, away from prying eyes.

On the ninth day, take the doll and the black cloth and bury it near a cemetery. Alternately, you can burn the doll and throw the ashes in a cemetery. Or, you may keep the doll and remove the parchment paper and nine pins from the doll and either bury them in or near a cemetery or burn and throw the ashes in or near a cemetery. If you keep the doll for future use, you may only use it for the same person, and you must keep it wrapped up and away from view, except when you wish to speak to your enemy through it.

Psalm 55

Have mercy on me, O God, for man hath trodden me under foot; all the day long he hath afflicted me fighting against me.

My enemies have trodden on me all the day long; for they are many that make war against me.

From the height of the day I shall fear: but I will trust in thee. **The height of the day...** That is, even at noonday, when the sun is the highest, I am still in danger.

In God I will praise my words, in God I have put my trust: I will not fear what flesh can do against me. **My words...** The words or promises God has made in my favour.

All the day long they detested my words: all their thoughts were against me unto evil.

They will dwell and hide themselves: they will watch my heel. As they have waited for my soul,

For nothing shalt thou save them: in thy anger thou shalt break the people in pieces. O God, **For nothing shalt thou save them...** That is, since they lie in wait to ruin my soul, thou shalt for no consideration favour or assist them, but execute thy justice upon them.

I have declared to thee my life: thou hast set me tears in thy sight, As also in thy promise.

Then shall my enemies be turned back. In what day soever I shall call upon thee, behold I know thou art my God.

Voodoo Dolls

In God will I praise the word, in the Lord will I praise his speech. In God have I hoped, I will not fear what man can do to me.
In me, O God, are vows to thee, which I will pay, praises to thee:
Because thou hast delivered my soul from death, my feet from falling: that I may please in the sight of God, in the light of the living.

Keep a Big Man Down Spell

This spell is designed to knock someone down a notch or two after they have gotten too big for their britches, like rich and arrogant. For this ritual you will need:

Blue candle
Black pen
Piece of paper
Bitter aloes
Cayenne pepper
Black poppet doll
Black thread
Black lace

Put the blue candle on your altar and light it. Write your target's name on a slip of paper with black ink. Take a small black poppet doll and rip open its back and put in the paper with the name along with some bitter aloes and cayenne pepper. Sew the rip up again with the black thread. Tie the hands of the doll behind its back and make a black veil from the lace and tie it over the face. Make a knot behind it so that the person it represents will be blind and always do stupid things to keep from progressing. Place the doll in a kneeling position in a dark corner where it won't be disturbed. Your target will be frustrated as long as the doll is not disturbed.

A Simple Ritual for Chango

Chango is the Voodoo deity of fire, thunder, power, wars, and lightening. He is also the symbol for sensual pleasure. Chango is the loa that can help you gain power over others, defeat your enemies, and achieve victory over all difficulties.

To use Chango, you should construct an altar for him. He prefers to be on a fireplace mantel, or on your business desk. His altar should be constructed using the following elements:

Patron saint: St. Barbara, St. Jerome
Day and number: Friday, 6
Country and owned places: Trinidad, sky, trees
Cloth and Bead colors: Red and white
Favorite animals and objects: Horses, rams, turtles, pheasants, machete, wood, double axe
Favorite food: apples, yams, corn, and peppers
Planets: Sun and Mars
Places in the house: Fireplace, business desk
Ritual greeting: Kaguo, Kabiosile

Use Chango as a focusing tool for the purpose you seek. First, light a red candle. Concentrate on the outcome you wish to occur and ask Chango for assistance in creating this change. Make an offering for three days

Voodoo Dolls

following your request. Appropriate offerings for Chango include any of his favorite foods, animals, and objects.

Voodoo Doll Banish and Hex Spell

Personalize a Voodoo poppet, labeling it with your rival's name photograph, and adding any intimate items you might have on hand.

1. Put the poppet inside a shoebox or paper bag.
2. Sprinkle it with Lost and Away Powder (made from crossroads dirt and graveyard dirt from three criminals).
3. Gently melt some black wax in a double boiler and pour it over the poppet.
4. Sprinkle the poppet with more Lost and Away powder before the wax hardens.
5. Bury the poppet in the ground far away from you home. Visit the poppet's grave once a week for nine weeks and sprinkle with more Lost and Away powder.

Your rival should be too preoccupied with their own problems to bother you anymore.

SPELL TO DOMINATE

This spell is based on hoodoo foot track magic.

1. Gather the dirt from your target's complete footprint.
2. Dampen with War Water combined with your own urine.
3. Create a human figure from the dirt, adding intimate items from your target, or add a slip of paper with the target's name on it.
4. Wrap a piece of red thread around the doll and pierce it with a nail.

The person it represents will now be under your command.

GAMBLER'S SPELL

This spell involves the creation of a lucky charm poppet for drawing good fortune in games of chance. For this spell you will need:

Green or money print fabric
Gold cloth
Several lucky charms like horseshoes, wishbone, four leaf clovers, dice, cards, etc.
Dried catnip, parsley, basil, and eucalyptus
Fool's gold
Fast Luck Oil
Play money

1. Lay out your green or money print fabric.
2. Cut out a human form either free form or using one of the patterns in this book.
3. Embellish the outside of the doll with as many lucky charms as you can. You can also draw lucky symbols on the doll if you wish.
4. Sew three sides together leaving a hole for stuffing the doll.
5. Fill the doll with the dried herbs and a piece of Fool's gold.
6. Finish sewing up the doll.
7. Continue to embellish with tiny charms until you are satisfied.
8. Anoint the doll with Fast Luck oil.
9. Place the finished doll on top of a piece of gold cloth along with lots of play money. Roll everything up, rolling towards you.

Voodoo Dolls

10. Pin everything together and keep in your home safe or close to where you keep your money.

Before gambling, anoint your doll with fast luck oil, and ask it for good luck.

GOSSIP SPELLS

These spells are used to prevent gossip, slander, and general verbal harassment.

Shut Your Mouth Spell

For this spell you will need the following items:

Black candle
Command and compel oil
Black Voodoo doll
Wax
Piece of dumb cane (wear gloves while handing this)

1. Dress a black candle with Command and Compel oil.
2. While it burns, make a Voodoo doll out of black cloth to represent the person who is spreading lies about you.
3. When you are finished making the doll, make a slit where the mouth should be and stuff a piece of dumb cane into the slit.
4. Dribble wax over the mouth of the Voodoo doll to seal in the cane and seal the mouth shut.

5. Bury the doll in a place in the woods far away from your home in a secluded area.

Leave the doll, don't look back, and never return.

Slippery Elm Banish Gossip Voodoo Doll Spell

Slippery elm is a common ingredient in sough syrups as it is soothing to the throat. This spell uses those properties to stop a person from speaking badly about you. For this spell you will need:

Slippery elm

2 sticks

Yellow strips of cloth

Cauldron, fireplace, or outdoor fire

1. Make a fire.
2. Burn slippery elm in the fire.
3. As the fire burns, take the two sticks and make a cross as if you were making a Voodoo doll.
4. begin wrapping the crossed sticks with the yellow fabric, tying knots as you go, concentrating all of your energy into stopping the gossip.
5. When you are done wrapping the doll and all of your frustrations are wrapped in the doll, throw the doll into the fire and watch it burn.

HEALING SPELLS

Doll forms have been used in rituals throughout time to transform illness into health and to stop disease.

Voodoo Dolls

Assyrian Healing Doll Spell

This spell is based in ancient Assyrian magic and is designed to restore a person to good health. It requires invocation and should not be performed by the inexperienced. It requires two people to perform this spell. One person will summon the Spirit of Disease and Illness, and the other person is the one who is ailing. For this ritual you will need:

Voodoo doll in the likeness of the sick person created out of wax or clay with a personal effect of the sick person attached to the doll
2 Fish charms
7 little winged figures
Sandalwood incense
Drum or drumming music
lime

1. Begin by burning some sandalwood incense on an altar and playing some heavy drumming music.
2. Create a protective circle out of flour. Sprinkle lime juice on the flour .This is where the ill person will stand or lay. Place 7 winged figures around the circle.
3. Spend a few minutes feeling the rhythm of the drums and focusing your intent.
4. Attach a fish charm to the sick person and another to the doll.
5. Place the Voodoo doll next to the incense on the altar.
6. Say: *I have completed the magic circle. I have surrounded them with the juice of a lime. With the flour of the corn god, the tabu of the great gods, I have surrounded them. I have set for the seven of them, the mighty winged, a figure of Nergal at their heads.*

7. Place the sick person in the magic circle and sprinkle them 7 times with holy water.
8. As you sprinkle the sick person with holy water, repeat the following incantation: *All that is evil that exists in the body of (name), may it be carried off with the water of his body, the washings from his hands, and may the river carry it away downstream.*
9. Address the Disease Spirit and command it to leave the sick person. *I give you this doll in which to reside, instead of (name the sick person). Let the flesh be of your flesh, the blood be of your blood. Hold it. Let the heart be of your heart, Hold it.*
10. As soon as it is evident that the disease spirit has left the body of the sick person, take the doll immediately from the premises and bury it far away from your home or burn it in a fire.
11. Both people in the ritual should take a cleansing bath following this ritual.

Basic Voodoo Doll Healing Spell with Pins

Make or buy a Voodoo doll dressed in white cloth. Light a white candle. Anoint the Voodoo doll with Yoruban Babaluye Healing oil (see recipe below) in the areas that are in need of healing, and anoint yourself in a likewise fashion. Using white tipped straight pins, insert the pins in these same areas while reciting the prayer to St. Lazarus.

Yoruban Babaluye Healing Oil

Combine oil of Rosemary, oil of Wormwood and Sage Oil to a base of grapeseed or almond oil. Add to the oil Cundiamor and Sesame Seeds to honor Babaluye and to promote health and healing.

Voodoo Dolls

Prayer to St. Lazarus

"Dear patron and assistant of the poor and sick. With this prayer I request your assistance, and with the aid of the Holy Spirit may the Lord always protect me during sickness or in health. St. Lazarus, give me the strength to overcome all the temptations on earth, in the name of the Father, the Son and the Holy Spirit. Amen."

SPELL FOR JUSTICE

This spell is for court cases in which you have to defend yourself from an adversary. Be absolutely sure that you are in the right; otherwise, the spell will benefit your adversary instead.

1. On the night before your court case, fashion a Voodoo doll to represent each of your adversaries.
2. Personalize each doll with a photo or some other identifier attached to the doll.
3. Place the doll on a clean white cloth.
4. Anoint the doll with Command and Compel and Court case oils.
5. Sprinkle crushed Vervain on top of the doll and recite psalm 7 nine times.
6. Wrap the doll inside the cloth and hide it in a discreet place where no one will disturb it.

Psalm 7 (King James Version)

O LORD my God, in thee do I put my trust: save me from all them that persecute me, and deliver me:

Lest he tear my soul like a lion, rending it in pieces, while there is none to deliver.

O LORD my God, If I have done this; if there be iniquity in my hands;

If I have rewarded evil unto him that was at peace with me; (yea, I have delivered him that without cause is mine enemy)

Let the enemy persecute my soul, and take it; yea, let him tread down my life upon the earth, and lay mine honour in the dust. Selah.

Arise, O LORD, in thine anger, lift up thyself because of the rage of mine enemies: and awake for me to the judgment that thou hast commanded.

So shall the congregation of the people compass thee about: for their sakes therefore return thou on high.

The LORD shall judge the people: judge me, O LORD, according to my righteousness, and according to mine integrity that is in me.

Oh let the wickedness of the wicked come to an end; but establish the just: for the righteous God trieth the hearts and reins.

My defence is of God, which saveth the upright in heart.

God judgeth the righteous, and God is angry with the wicked every day.

If he turn not, he will whet his sword; he hath bent his bow, and made it ready.

He hath also prepared for him the instruments of death; he ordaineth his arrows against the persecutors.

Behold, he travaileth with iniquity, and hath conceived mischief, and brought forth falsehood.

He made a pit, and digged it, and is fallen into the ditch which he made.

His mischief shall return upon his own head, and his violent dealing shall come down upon his own pate.

I will praise the LORD according to his righteousness: and will sing praise to the name of the LORD most high.

LOVE AND ATTRACTION SPELLS

Love and attraction spells are best performed during a waxing or full moon. This is the best time for drawing someone close.

Commanding Doll Spell

Purchase an all purpose Voodoo doll or make a Voodoo doll to represent the target of your intentions. Then do the following:

1. Write your beloved's name on a piece of parchment paper.
2. Attach it to your Voodoo doll like a name tag.
3. Anoint the doll with Command and Compel Oil. Lay it on a piece of red silk or satin, and sprinkle it with come to me powder.
4. Chant:

   I command you, I compel you.
   I command you, I compel you.
   I've covered you with powder.
   I command you, I compel you,
   I command you, I compel you
   Hear my voice!
   I command you, I compel you.
   Return to me now!
   Thus very instant, this very minute, this very hour!

Repeat for three consecutive nights. Following the third repetition of the entire ritual, wrap the doll in the silk, and hide it in a dark closet or secret space.

Love Drawing Voodoo Doll Spell

Create a pink or red Voodoo doll or poppet. Every Friday during a waxing moon, sprinkle cinnamon on the doll while saying the following:

Let the cinnamon in my hand I turn to fire in the heart of the male/female I am looking for. Let her/him have no peace of mind until she/he is with me.

Repeat this spell 3 Fridays in a row. On the 3rd time, say the following: *Let the cinnamon in my hand I turn to fire in the heart of the male/female I am looking for. He/she will have no peace of mind until she/he is with me.*

The person you are looking for should appear within the next few weeks. As with any spell, you must watch for the signs. If the person does not appear, repeat the spell. You may repeat the entire spell three times before throwing in the towel.

Love Effigies

Create two hearts out of wax and baptize them with the names of the two lovers. Pin the hearts together with three red pins. Give the heart effigies to the person who is seeking love and tell them to hold the wax hearts to their own heart while focusing on being with their lover.

Oshun Love Spell

The following ritual invokes the spirit of Oshun. Oshun is the Santeria goddess of love, art, and dance. She also provides emotional stability.

Ideally, you will begin at your altar. It is advisable to have altar candles (yellow, green, or pink) and spiritual incense burning (cinnamon) at the time of use. To begin, you will need to ask Papa Legba to open the gates to the spirit world so that you can ask Oshun for a favor. To do so, recite the following three times:

Voodoo Dolls

Odu Legba, Papa Legba, open the door, Your children are waiting.
Papa Legba, open the door, your children await.

Focus on your Voodoo doll, getting a clear image in your mind of the change you seek. Oshun is particularly useful for improving love, happiness, and emotional strength. Concentrate on the outcome you wish to occur and greet Oshun with the appropriate ritual greeting:

Ori Ye Ye O!

You may now ask Oshun for assistance in creating the change you seek. You may write a petition if you wish. Make an offering for three days following your request. Appropriate offerings include lighting a special candle, placing a small plate of food from your dinner on her altar, or flowers. Oshun is particularly fond of cinnamon, honey, oranges, pumpkins, gold, mirrors, and French pastries. Her favorite colors are yellow, green, and coral, her favorite day is Thursday, and her favorite number is the number 5. Be creative! When you are finished, place Oshun in your kitchen or in the bedroom as these are the best places in the home for her.

Oshun Love and Prosperity Spell

For this spell, you need the following ingredients:

Orange rind
Dried orange leaves
Cinnamon
Brown sugar
An iron pot
Oshun Voodoo Doll

Place the ingredients in the pot and burn them. Smother the fire and leave the smoldering mixture smoking heavily. Offer the incense to Oshun and say:

Oshun oguao mi inle oshun igua iya mio igua iko bo si iya mi guasi iya mi omo y alorde oguo mi inle ashe oshun.

Alternately, you may respectfully pray to Oshun in your own language for the love and prosperity that you need.

New Orleans Voodoo Knot Doll Love Spell

It is said that followers of Marie Laveau would create a knotted cord to bind two dolls to cast a love spell on two people. For this spell you need a cord about two feet long that you will tie seven knots about one inch apart from each other and two dolls representing the two lovers.

1. Take the cord and tie the first knot in the middle of the cord. While tying the knot say *"May (name the two lovers) be bound to each other from this moment on. May their love remain in this circle that binds them."*
2. Tie the second knot about an inch to the right of the first knot and say: *"The love between (name the lovers) will endure with the strength of steel."*
3. Tie a knot about an inch to the left of the first knot and say *"(Name the lovers) will not be able to part from each other even though their passion may fluctuate in intensity."*
4. Tie the fourth knot to the right and say *"May all good spirits and the Holy Light keep the image of one in the heart and mind of the other."*
5. Tie the fifth knot to the left and say *"May (name the lovers) always be faithful to each other."*

Voodoo Dolls

6. Tie the sixth knot to the right and say *"(Name the lovers) will have and express their love and affection to each other and only to each other."*
7. Tie the seventh knot to the left and say *"The two lovers (name the lovers) will always stand within the circle of their love and happiness, never to be broken by any power on Earth."*

Once all of the knots are tied and the incantation is complete, bind the two dolls together with the knotted cord and tie the two ends of the cord together. Place the Knot Love Doll under the bed for seven nights. On the seventh day, the dolls should be hidden in a secret place where they will not be disturbed or burned as an offering to good spirits.

Pierced Heart Doll Spell

Pierce the heart of a Voodoo love doll with a red and a blue pin in such a way that they cross each other. Then chant:

It is not this doll alone I stick
But [Name]'s heart I prick
Whether he/she be asleep or awake
I'll have him/her come to me and of love make!

Twenty Seven Day Paper Voodoo Doll Spell

1. Cut out a paper Voodoo doll.
2. Write your lover's name on the paper Voodoo doll nine times.
3. Cross over each name with your own.
4. Place the paper Voodoo doll in a saucer or plate and cover it with sugar.

5. Stick a blue birthday candle in the center of the sugar, make a wish and burn the candle, but don't blow it out. Keep the dish with the sugar, paper Voodoo doll, and any wax drippings.
6. Add a fresh birthday candle the next day. Repeat for a total of nine days - nine blue birthday candles in total.
7. If your lover is not back by the ninth day, burn the sugar and the paper.
8. Start again the next day, repeating the entire 9 day ritual with fresh materials. If your lover is not back, burn the materials again.
9. Try it again for another nine days.

Three times is the charm. If you lover is not back after repeating this ritual three times, he or she won't be and it is best to move on.

Voodoo Virility Doll Spell

Voodoo virility dolls are created for enhancing relationships, love, sex, and passion. For this spell you will need:

Voodoo Virility Doll (anatomically correct doll with stiff penis)
Small piece of parchment paper
Glass of milk
Honey
Magnetic sand
Piece of red flannel
Sinew or string
Mojo blend

Voodoo Dolls

1. Write your beloved's name on a piece of parchment paper. If you are not targeting one person in particular, simply write "women" or "virility" or "sex".
2. Sprinkle it with some of the magnetic sand (save some of the sand)
3. Attach it to your Voodoo doll with the red pin like a name tag. If you want love, attach it near his heart. If you want sex, passion, or virility, attach it near his penis.
4. Put three teaspoons of honey into the glass of milk and stir it up real good.
5. Raise your glass of milk as if in a toast and chant:

    I command you, I compel you.

    I command you, I compel you.

    I hold you near me for love (or sex).

    I command you, I compel you.

    I command you, I compel you.

    Hear my voice!

    I command you, I compel you.

    I am hard as a rock!

    I will be with you

    This very instant, this very minute, this very hour!
6. Drink the milk and honey.
7. Repeat for three consecutive days.

Following the third repetition of the entire ritual, place the mojo blend in the center of the red flannel and sprinkle with the remaining magnetic sand. Tie it up in a bundle with the piece of sinew real good and carry it with you to charge your virility. Proudly display the doll in your bedroom with his shirt up when you desire sex, with his shirt down when you need rest.

Wax Doll Summoning Spell

This spell is designed to draw a lover near. Perform during a waxing moon.

1. Make a wax image of your loved one, mixing into the wax some hair, saliva, semen, blood or whatever is available.
2. Prick your wedding finger with a needle.
3. Write the name of your lover on the forehead of the doll with the bloody pin.
4. Using four new needles prick the heart, groin, head, and lower back areas. Visualize your lover's growing desire for you with each prick.
5. Sprinkle the doll with powdered sugar.
6. Write a petition on a piece of parchment paper stating exactly what you want from your lover.
7. Burn the paper in a fire. In the remaining ashes, write the name of your lover with your finger.
8. Wrap the doll along with the ashes in a red cloth and keep under your mattress until your lover comes to you.

Poppet Bonding Spell

Create a poppet in pink or red. To create a relationship with the person you seek, you must first develop a relationship with the poppet. To do this, you need to name the poppet. Use this simple naming ritual:

Little doll, I made you and now I give you life
I name you (person's name)
His/Her body is your body

His/Her breath is your breath
His/Her passion is your passion
His/Her blood is your blood
Though separate you were
Now you are one.

WEALTH AND PROSPERITY SPELLS

Here are some spells you can do with your Voodoo doll to attract wealth and prosperity.

Mo' Money Spell

1. Cut out a Voodoo poppet doll from green material, preferably flannel.
2. Stuff it with Irish moss and dill weed, then sew it up and decorate as you see fit.
3. Tell the doll your wish is for more money and ask for advice in the dreamtime. Then pay attention to your dreams for signs.

Money Doll

Create a Voodoo poppet out of green cloth using gold thread. Stuff the doll with spirit money, alfalfa, and mint. On one piece of spirit money, write a petition: *I require (fill in the blank) amount of money plus some extra. I need this immediately to meet my needs.* Place inside the doll. Anoint the doll with Fast Luck Oil. Wrap the doll in green or gold cloth. Anoint the doll every day until your petition has been fulfilled, then burn the doll. Repeat as needed.

Spells and Rituals

Wealth and Prosperity Voodoo Doll Spell

1. Cut out a Voodoo poppet from green material. Sew it closed with gold thread, leaving a space for stuffing.
2. Make a stuffing of Irish moss, comfrey, and parsley. Add nine shiny pennies.
3. Write a note on a piece of parchment paper exactly the amount of money you need and when you need it. Fold and stuff the note inside the poppet. Sew the doll closed.
4. Use a money oil to dress the doll, such as Fast Luck Oil.
5. Wrap the doll in green or gold cloth.
6. Anoint the doll daily until your need has been met, and then burn the poppet.

VOODOO DOLL CURSES

How can I curse thee? Let me count the ways...hex, bind, curse, jinx, trick, cross, goofer ... all ways of saying something very similar in the Voodoo hoodoo vernacular. But just what is a curse, exactly? And what's more important to many I am sure, just how does one go about puttin' the bad mojo on someone?

A curse is the effective action of some power, or result from a spell or prayer, asking that a god, natural force, or spirit bring misfortune to someone. In Voodoo, to perform such a "trick" is to work the left hand of Voodoo. They are considered black magic spells because they are concerned with hurting, harming, goofering, jinxing, or hot footing enemies.

Voodoo Dolls

On the other hand, certain types of spells can be used to repel negative energy, to keep a perpetrator from hurting someone, or for driving away bad neighbors.

At the risk of sounding completely redundant, please note that the following information is meant for educational purposes only. You are advised to think very seriously before attempting to perform any of the spells provided and to consider the Law of Three, which states that everything you do, will come back to you threefold. Proceed at your own risk.

Basic Pins and Needles Voodoo Doll Hex

1. Create a Voodoo doll or poppet to represent the target of your intentions.
2. Add some of the target's clothing or personal effects, hair or nail clippings, whatever you may have and wrap it into the body of the doll.
3. Prick the doll with a needle in a series of three or nine as the spirit moves you.

Death Curse

Create a poppet out of wax or clay. Write the name of your victim into the wax or clay with a pin. Pierce the doll with a thorn or needle in the area of the body that you wish to inflict pain. Wrap the doll in a cloth shroud and pray over it as if it was a person who just died and you were performing the death rites at their funeral. When you have finished the death rites, bury the doll in a spot where you are certain the person will walk.

Magic Doll Spell from the Great Book of St. Cyprian

The following is a Voodoo doll spell taken from the Great Book of Saint Cyprian written by O Antigo Livro de São Cipriano: Capa de Aço and Translated from Portuguese by Ray Vogensen.

The Great Book of Saint Cyprian is a book that deals with the occult. It was taken from Portugal to Brazil and became widely used in popular religion, especially Umbanda and Candomble. Saint Cyprian is the patron saint of witches, conjurers, root doctors, and spiritual workers, both good and evil.

Many consider it a sin to possess it or even to touch the book. Some owners of book shops keep it chained inside a box. In Portugal, it is believed that reading the book back to front will attract the devil.

Spell to do Evil using Two Dolls

Make two cloth dolls, connecting one to the other, tying them so that they appear to be embracing; then put in five nails in the following parts:

1st nail, in the head, going all the way through, saying the following: So and so (the name of the person to whom you want to do evil), I (say your name), nail you and tie and stab your body, just as I stab, tie and nail your figure.

2nd nail, in the chest, all the way through, saying the following: So and so (the name of the person to whom you want to do evil) I swear to you, under the power of Lucifer and Satan, that from now on you will not have an hour of health.

3rd nail, in the stomach. So and so, I swear to you, under the power of evil magic, that from now on you will not have one moment of peace.

4th nail, in the legs. So and so, I swear to you, under the power of Maria Padilha, (see more below) that from now on you will be under this spell.

5th nail, in the feet. So and so, I nail you and tie you from head to toe, by the power of the sorcerer's magic. With this the bewitched person will never have a moment of good health.

Maria Padilha - whose name means Queen of Fire, is an entity of light that works for good. She lived a long time ago in France, and was the madam of a house of prostitution (Cabaré), all the men she had, in each one of her incarnations, which were seven, are with her in the spirit world. There is a prophecy that says that in the year 2000 Maria Padilha, queen of the queens, will step on the Orixás. The Orixás will worship her since her mission is to convert the man that she loves (Lucifer, angel of darkness) to the world of light. They will enter the house of God dressed in white. She will sit alongside Jesus and he at the feet of Christ. Maria Padilha will save 7000 souls and will give 7000 to the flames of hell.

Voodoo Doll Curse from the Necronomicon

Chant over a doll of wax as it burns in a cauldron to cause sickness in another:

AZAG galra sagbi mu unna te
NAMTAR galra zibi mu unna te
UTUK XUL gubi mu unna te
ALA XUL gabi mu unna te
GIDIM XUL ibbi mu unna te
GALLA XUL kadbi mu unna te

DINGIR XUL girbi mu unna te

I minabi-ene tashbi aba aba-andibbi-esh!

"And in these things they took great delight, and still do where they are to be found at their shrines of loathsomeness."

Voodoo Doll Curse Herbal Blend Recipe

To make an herbal blend that will be used as stuffing in a Voodoo poppet doll that will be used for break up rituals, cursing or crossing, blend equal amounts of the following in a bowl:

Witches' grass
Blood Root
Patchouli

Anoint the mixture with Black Arts Oil. Write the name of your target on a piece of parchment paper with Bat's Blood ink, anoint with Black Arts oil, and place inside a Voodoo poppet. Stuff the doll with the herbal curse blend. Place the doll where your enemy will find it, or bury the doll near their home, or in the woods far away from your home.

To Cross an Enemy

For this spell, you will need:

One black poppet doll (male or female as is appropriate)
Black candle
Commanding Oil
Crossing Oil

Voodoo Dolls

Black Arts Oil
Crossing Powder
Revenge Oil
Bend Over Oil
A small box
Black Cotton Fabric
Cotton Twine
Nine copper pennies
A small bottle of rum
A red pen
Black headed straight pin

Using the red pin, write the name of your enemy on a piece of parchment paper and attach to the black poppet doll with a black headed straight pin. Anoint the doll each one of the oils. Gently dust the doll with the Crossing Powder by taking a spoonful of the powder and blowing gently onto the poppet.

Light the black candle for 9 minutes each day for nine days. While the candle burns, focus your thoughts and will on your target. After the ninth day, place the remainder of the candle along with the poppet in a small box. Wrap the box in black cloth. Tie it with twine or sinew. Take it to the cemetery and bury it. Pay the spirits of death with whom you are burying the box nine cents and a small bottle of rum. Walk away without looking back.

To Keep a Person Frustrated and Unsuccessful

Make a poppet out of black cloth. Write the name of the victim on parchment paper, make a slit in the back of the doll, and place the paper inside. Put cayenne pepper in the slit with the paper and sew up the doll with black thread. Tie the dolls hands at the back and place it in a kneeling position in a corner somewhere where it won't be disturbed. As long as the doll is undisturbed, the person represented will be kept down. You can abuse the doll in any way you like and the person it represents will be similarly affected.

CHAPTER 11:
Using the Psalms in Voodoo Doll Magick

Voodoo dolls are most often used as focusing tools in meditation and prayer. You may use the following psalms with your Voodoo doll by reciting the psalm while holding your Voodoo doll in a manner that gives you comfort. You will not need to look up the specific psalms in your personal bible, as I have provided them for you.

The psalms I have provided are from the King James Version (KJV) of the bible. The KJV is public domain in the United States. Use an all purpose Voodoo doll with the psalms, or use the specific ones indicated.

Psalm for Successful Business

Psalm #8: Procure an Oya Voodoo doll. Oya is the loa of the marketplace and consummate business woman. Alternately, make a Voodoo doll and baptize it in the name of **Rechmial**. As you hold the doll to your heart, pray this psalm three days in a row after sunset for a successful business venture or to procure the goodwill in your business transactions. While praying, be mindful of the Holy name of Rechmial, which signifies strong and merciful God of love, grace, and mercy. After praying the Psalm #8, thinking the name Rechmial, also say the following prayer over a small quantity of olive oil: *"May it please thee, Oh, Rechmial Eel, to grant that I may obtain love, grace, and favor in the eyes of men according to they holy will. Amen! Selah!"*

Psalm 8 (King James Version)

O LORD, our Lord, how excellent is thy name in all the earth! who hast set thy glory above the heavens.

Out of the mouth of babes and sucklings hast thou ordained strength because of thine enemies, that thou mightest still the enemy and the avenger.

When I consider thy heavens, the work of thy fingers, the moon and the stars, which thou hast ordained;

What is man, that thou art mindful of him? and the son of man, that thou visitest him?

For thou hast made him a little lower than the angels, and hast crowned him with glory and honour.

Thou madest him to have dominion over the works of thy hands; thou hast put all things under his feet:

All sheep and oxen, yea, and the beasts of the field;

The fowl of the air, and the fish of the sea, and whatsoever passeth through the paths of the seas.

O LORD our Lord, how excellent is thy name in all the earth!

Psalm to Stop Persecution

Psalm #11: For this psalm, use an Ochosi or Manman Brigit Voodoo doll. Both are good for matters of justice. Alternately, make a Voodoo doll and baptize it in the name of **Pele.** To put a stop to persecution in all forms, hold the doll to your heart, and pray this Psalm daily in devotion keeping

Voodoo Dolls

constantly in mind the holy name of Pele, that all conspiracies against you may be set aside. After praying Psalm #11, close with the following prayer: *"Adorable, might, and holy God Pele, with thee is advice, action, and power, and only thou canst work wonders. Turn away from me all that is evil, and protect me from the persecution of evil ones, for the sake of the Great Name Pele. Amen. Sela."*

Psalm 11 (King James Version)

In the LORD put I my trust: how say ye to my soul, Flee as a bird to your mountain?

For, lo, the wicked bend their bow, they make ready their arrow upon the string, that they may privily shoot at the upright in heart.

If the foundations be destroyed, what can the righteous do?

The LORD is in his holy temple, the LORD's throne is in heaven: his eyes behold, his eyelids try, the children of men.

The LORD trieth the righteous: but the wicked and him that loveth violence his soul hateth.

Upon the wicked he shall rain snares, fire and brimstone, and an horrible tempest: this shall be the portion of their cup.

For the righteous LORD loveth righteousness; his countenance doth behold the upright.

Psalm to Stop all Libel

Psalm #35: Make and use a Voodoo doll baptized in the name of **Tehom**. To stop all evil, slanderous libel being maliciously spread about you, hold the doll to your heart, and pray this Psalm daily and they will cause you no evil. Use the holy name Tehom.

Psalm 35 (King James Version)

Plead my cause, O LORD, with them that strive with me: fight against them that fight against me.

Take hold of shield and buckler, and stand up for mine help.

Draw out also the spear, and stop the way against them that persecute me: say unto my soul, I am thy salvation.

Let them be confounded and put to shame that seek after my soul: let them be turned back and brought to confusion that devise my hurt.

Let them be as chaff before the wind: and let the angel of the LORD chase them.

Let their way be dark and slippery: and let the angel of the LORD persecute them.

For without cause have they hid for me their net in a pit, which without cause they have digged for my soul.

Let destruction come upon him at unawares; and let his net that he hath hid catch himself: into that very destruction let him fall.

And my soul shall be joyful in the LORD: it shall rejoice in his salvation.

All my bones shall say, LORD, who is like unto thee, which deliverest the poor from him that is too strong for him, yea, the poor and the needy from him that spoileth him?

False witnesses did rise up; they laid to my charge things that I knew not.

They rewarded me evil for good to the spoiling of my soul.

But as for me, when they were sick, my clothing was sackcloth: I humbled my soul with fasting; and my prayer returned into mine own bosom.

I behaved myself as though he had been my friend or brother: I bowed down heavily, as one that mourneth for his mother.

Voodoo Dolls

But in mine adversity they rejoiced, and gathered themselves together: yea, the abjects gathered themselves together against me, and I knew it not; they did tear me, and ceased not:

With hypocritical mockers in feasts, they gnashed upon me with their teeth.

Lord, how long wilt thou look on? rescue my soul from their destructions, my darling from the lions.

I will give thee thanks in the great congregation: I will praise thee among much people.

Let not them that are mine enemies wrongfully rejoice over me: neither let them wink with the eye that hate me without a cause.

For they speak not peace: but they devise deceitful matters against them that are quiet in the land.

Yea, they opened their mouth wide against me, and said, Aha, aha, our eye hath seen it.

This thou hast seen, O LORD: keep not silence: O Lord, be not far from me.

Stir up thyself, and awake to my judgment, even unto my cause, my God and my Lord.

Judge me, O LORD my God, according to thy righteousness; and let them not rejoice over me.

Let them not say in their hearts, Ah, so would we have it: let them not say, We have swallowed him up.

Let them be ashamed and brought to confusion together that rejoice at mine hurt: let them be clothed with shame and dishonour that magnify themselves against me.

Let them shout for joy, and be glad, that favour my righteous cause: yea, let them say continually, Let the LORD be magnified, which hath pleasure in the prosperity of his servant.

And my tongue shall speak of thy righteousness and of thy praise all the day long.

Psalm to Make Yourself Beloved

Psalm #47: If you wish to be respected, beloved, well received in any and all situations, pray this Psalm seven times daily with an all-purpose Voodoo doll.

Psalm 47 (King James Version)

O clap your hands, all ye people; shout unto God with the voice of triumph.

For the LORD most high is terrible; he is a great King over all the earth.

He shall subdue the people under us, and the nations under our feet.

He shall choose our inheritance for us, the excellency of Jacob whom he loved. Selah.

God is gone up with a shout, the LORD with the sound of a trumpet.

Sing praises to God, sing praises: sing praises unto our King, sing praises.

For God is the King of all the earth: sing ye praises with understanding.

God reigneth over the heathen: God sitteth upon the throne of his holiness.

The princes of the people are gathered together, even the people of the God of Abraham: for the shields of the earth belong unto God: he is greatly exalted.

Psalm to Make Your Home Lucky

Psalm #61: For this psalm, use a good luck or money Voodoo doll. If you are moving into a new home, hold the doll to your heart and repeat this Psalm in the home, just before moving in, trusting in the name of **Schaddel**, and you will experience good fortune and luck in the new home. For your present home, clean from top to bottom with plain spring water, leave the home and then return, and repeat this Psalm seven days in a row.

Psalm 61 (King James Version)

Hear my cry, O God; attend unto my prayer.

From the end of the earth will I cry unto thee, when my heart is overwhelmed: lead me to the rock that is higher than I.

For thou hast been a shelter for me, and a strong tower from the enemy.

I will abide in thy tabernacle for ever: I will trust in the covert of thy wings. Selah.

For thou, O God, hast heard my vows: thou hast given me the heritage of those that fear thy name.

Thou wilt prolong the king's life: and his years as many generations.

He shall abide before God for ever: O prepare mercy and truth, which may preserve him.

So will I sing praise unto thy name for ever, that I may daily perform my vows.

Psalms for Making Peace between Husband and Wife

Psalms #45 and 46 – Create a Voodoo doll to represent your scolding wife. Pronounce the 45th Psalm over pure olive oil, and anoint your body with it, and the body of the doll. This will make your wife more loving and friendlier in the future. Wrap the doll in white cloth and place under the bed or mattress. If your wife is angry with you and you would like to make love to her and create harmony between you, pray the 46th Psalm over olive oil, and anoint your wife thoroughly with it, and, it is said, married love will again return.

Psalm 45 (King James Version)

My heart is inditing a good matter: I speak of the things which I have made touching the king: my tongue is the pen of a ready writer.

Thou art fairer than the children of men: grace is poured into thy lips: therefore God hath blessed thee for ever.

Gird thy sword upon thy thigh, O most mighty, with thy glory and thy majesty.

And in thy majesty ride prosperously because of truth and meekness and righteousness; and thy right hand shall teach thee terrible things.

Thine arrows are sharp in the heart of the king's enemies; whereby the people fall under thee.

Thy throne, O God, is for ever and ever: the sceptre of thy kingdom is a right sceptre.

Thou lovest righteousness, and hatest wickedness: therefore God, thy God, hath anointed thee with the oil of gladness above thy fellows.

All thy garments smell of myrrh, and aloes, and cassia, out of the ivory palaces, whereby they have made thee glad.

Kings' daughters were among thy honourable women: upon thy right hand did stand the queen in gold of Ophir.

Hearken, O daughter, and consider, and incline thine ear; forget also thine own people, and thy father's house;

So shall the king greatly desire thy beauty: for he is thy Lord; and worship thou him.

And the daughter of Tyre shall be there with a gift; even the rich among the people shall intreat thy favour.

The king's daughter is all glorious within: her clothing is of wrought gold.

She shall be brought unto the king in raiment of needlework: the virgins her companions that follow her shall be brought unto thee.

With gladness and rejoicing shall they be brought: they shall enter into the king's palace.

Instead of thy fathers shall be thy children, whom thou mayest make princes in all the earth.

I will make thy name to be remembered in all generations: therefore shall the people praise thee for ever and ever.

Psalm 46 (King James Version)

God is our refuge and strength, a very present help in trouble.

Therefore will not we fear, though the earth be removed, and though the mountains be carried into the midst of the sea;

Though the waters thereof roar and be troubled, though the mountains shake with the swelling thereof. Selah.

There is a river, the streams whereof shall make glad the city of God, the holy place of the tabernacles of the most High.

God is in the midst of her; she shall not be moved: God shall help her, and that right early.

The heathen raged, the kingdoms were moved: he uttered his voice, the earth melted.

The LORD of hosts is with us; the God of Jacob is our refuge. Selah.

Come, behold the works of the LORD, what desolations he hath made in the earth.

He maketh wars to cease unto the end of the earth; he breaketh the bow, and cutteth the spear in sunder; he burneth the chariot in the fire.

Be still, and know that I am God: I will be exalted among the heathen, I will be exalted in the earth.

The LORD of hosts is with us; the God of Jacob is our refuge. Selah.

Psalm for Safe Travel at Night

Psalm #121 – If you travel alone by night, pray this Psalm reverently seven times with a Gran Bwa Voodoo doll, and you will be safe from all accidents and evil occurrences.

Psalm 121 (King James Version)

I will lift up mine eyes unto the hills, from whence cometh my help.

My help cometh from the LORD, which made heaven and earth.

He will not suffer thy foot to be moved: he that keepeth thee will not slumber.

Behold, he that keepeth Israel shall neither slumber nor sleep.

The LORD is thy keeper: the LORD is thy shade upon thy right hand.

The sun shall not smite thee by day, nor the moon by night.

The LORD shall preserve thee from all evil: he shall preserve thy soul.

The LORD shall preserve thy going out and thy coming in from this time forth, and even for evermore.

Psalm for Severe Headache or Backache

Psalm #3 -- Whosoever is subject to severe headache and backache, let him pray this Psalm over a small quantity of olive oil, [and] anoint the head or back while in prayer. This will afford immediate relief. You may use a white

Voodoo Dolls

Voodoo doll and white pins to pierce the doll in the places where healing and relief are needed.

Psalm 3 (King James Version)

Lord, how are they increased that trouble me! many are they that rise up against me.
Many there be which say of my soul, There is no help for him in God. Selah.
But thou, O LORD, art a shield for me; my glory, and the lifter up of mine head.
I cried unto the LORD with my voice, and he heard me out of his holy hill. Selah.
I laid me down and slept; I awaked; for the LORD sustained me.
I will not be afraid of ten thousands of people, that have set themselves against me round about.
Arise, O LORD; save me, O my God: for thou hast smitten all mine enemies upon the cheek bone; thou hast broken the teeth of the ungodly.
Salvation belongeth unto the LORD: thy blessing is upon thy people. Selah.

Psalm for a Repentant Liar

Psalm #132 -- If you have sworn to perform anything punctually, and notwithstanding your oath you neglect to perform your obligation, and in this manner have perjured yourself, you should, in order to avoid a future crime of a similar kind, pray this Psalm daily with profound reverence. Use a white Voodoo doll for this psalm.

Psalm 132 (King James Version)

Lord, remember David, and all his afflictions:

How he sware unto the LORD, and vowed unto the mighty God of Jacob;

Surely I will not come into the tabernacle of my house, nor go up into my bed;

I will not give sleep to mine eyes, or slumber to mine eyelids,

Until I find out a place for the LORD, an habitation for the mighty God of Jacob.

Lo, we heard of it at Ephratah: we found it in the fields of the wood.

We will go into his tabernacles: we will worship at his footstool.

Arise, O LORD, into thy rest; thou, and the ark of thy strength.

Let thy priests be clothed with righteousness; and let thy saints shout for joy.

For thy servant David's sake turn not away the face of thine anointed.

The LORD hath sworn in truth unto David; he will not turn from it; Of the fruit of thy body will I set upon thy throne.

If thy children will keep my covenant and my testimony that I shall teach them, their children shall also sit upon thy throne for evermore.

For the LORD hath chosen Zion; he hath desired it for his habitation.

This is my rest for ever: here will I dwell; for I have desired it.

I will abundantly bless her provision: I will satisfy her poor with bread.

I will also clothe her priests with salvation: and her saints shall shout aloud for joy.

There will I make the horn of David to bud: I have ordained a lamp for mine anointed.

His enemies will I clothe with shame: but upon himself shall his crown flourish.

CHAPTER 12:
Prayers to Use when Petitioning the Spirits with Voodoo Dolls

In this day and age of technology and instant gratification, we often forget how Spirit impacts out lives. Prayer is a way to focus our hearts, minds, and spirits to the unseen mysteries of the universe. With prayer, all things are possible. If you don't know any formal prayers, it does not matter. If you don't know how to pray, it doesn't matter. What is most important is that you speak with sincerity and speak from your heart.

One way in which African slaves could continue to practice their traditional religions was by shrouding the African spirits in elements of Catholicism. As a result, there are corresponding saints for each of the major deities or Seven African Powers. The Seven African Powers is a Hoodoo term that is used by practitioners of Santeria, New Orleans Voodoo, Candomble, and other religions. In Spanish, they are referred to as Las Sietes Potencias. If you know the saint that corresponds to the particular loa/Orisha, then you can use the prayer to the specific saints when working with your Voodoo doll. Following is a list of some of the major spirits (Loas/Orishas), their purpose, corresponding saints, and prayers.

Eleggua / Elegua/Papa Legba

Purpose: Messenger, Opener of the Way, Trickster, Gatekeeper to the Spirit World

Corresponding Saints: Saint Simon Peter, San Martin (Caballero), Saint Anthony (of Padua), El Nino de Atocha, Saint Expedite, Saint Michael the Archangel

Here are some specific prayers to use when working with your Papa Legba Voodoo Doll.

Prayers for Saint Anthony

Likened to Elegua/Legba and Ogun of Santeria/Voodoo traditions, Saint Anthony is known to answer the prayers of those seeking special favors. He is renowned for helping folks find lost things and people and assisting those who desire marriage.

St. Anthony can be summoned by saying the following:

Dear St. Anthony, I pray
Bring it back, without delay.

Or:

St. Anthony, St. Anthony
Please come down
Something is lost
And can't be found.

Unfailing Prayer to Saint Anthony

Blessed be God in His Angels and in His Saints.
O Holy St. Anthony, gentlest of Saints, your love for God
and Charity for His creatures made you worthy, when on
earth, to possess miraculous powers. Miracles waited on
your word, which you were ever ready to speak for those in
trouble or anxiety. Encouraged by this thought, I implore
of you to obtain for me (request). The answer to my prayer may require a
miracle. Even so, you are the saint of
Miracles.
O gentle and loving St. Anthony, whose heart was ever full
of human sympathy, whisper my petition into the ears of the
Sweet Infant Jesus, who loved to be folded in your arms, and
the gratitude of my heart will ever be yours.
Amen. (Say 13 Paters, Aves, and Glorias)

Obatalá

Purpose: Father-Mother of Humanity, Bringer of Peace and Harmony, Androgynous Sky King of the White Cloth

Corresponding saints: Our Lady of Mercy , Our Lady of Mt. Carmel

Here is a prayer to use when working with your Obatala Voodoo doll:

Prayer to our Lady of Mercy

(By St. Augustine of Hippo)
Blessed Virgin Mary,
Who can worthily repay you with praise
And thanks for having rescued a fallen world

By your generous consent!
Receive our gratitude,
And by your prayers obtain the pardon of our sins.
Take our prayers into the sanctuary of heaven
And enable them to make our peace with God.
Holy Mary, help the miserable,
Strengthen the discouraged,
Comfort the sorrowful,
Pray for your people,
Plead for the clergy,
Intercede for all women consecrated to God.
May all who venerate you
Feel now your help and protection.
Be ready to help us when we pray,
And bring back to us the answers to our prayers.
Make it your continual concern
To pray for the people of God,
For you were blessed by God
And were made worthy to bear the Redeemer of the world,
Who lives and reigns forever.
Amen.

Yemayá

Purpose: Spirit of Motherhood, the Ocean, and the Moon, Goddess of the Seven Seas

Corresponding saints: Our Lady of Regla Mary, Star of the Sea

Voodoo Dolls

Prayer to Yemayá

My Queen!

My Mother!

I give thee all myself, and, to show my devotion to thee, I consecrate to thee my eyes, my ears, my mouth, my heart, my entire self. Where-fore, O loving Mother, as I am thine own, keep me, defend me, as thy property and possession.

Oyá

Purpose: Female Warrior, Spirit of Wind, Storm, Thunder, and Magic, Mistress of the Marketplace

Corresponding Saints: Our Lady of Candelaria, Saint Catherine, Saint Theresa

Here is a prayer to use when working with your Oya Voodoo doll:

St. Theresa of the Child Jesus

O wondrous Saint Theresa of the Child Jesus, who, in thy brief earthly life, didst become a mirror of angelic purity, of courageous love and of wholehearted surrender to Almighty God, now that thou art enjoying the reward of thy virtues, turn thine eyes of mercy upon us who trust in thee. Obtain for us the grace to keep our hearts and minds pure and clean like unto thine, and to detest in all sincerity whatever might tarnish ever so slightly the luster of a virtue so sublime, a virtue that endears us to they heavenly Bridegroom. Ah, dear Saint, grant us to feel in every need the power of thy intercession; give us comfort in all the bitterness of this life and especially at its latter end, that we may be worthy to share eternal happiness with thee in paradise. Amen.

Oshun / Ochum

Purpose: Goddess of Love, Beauty, and Sexuality, Spirit of Fresh Water

Corresponding saints: Our Lady of Caridad del Cobre (Our Mother of Charity)

African Prayer to Oshun

Oshun, I bow to you!
You are very rich digging in the sand
To hide money there.
Oshun, I bow to you!
You are very beautiful
With your coral hair combs
And your cast copper jewelry.
Oshun, I bow to you!
You are very powerful
You have seized the crown
Look at you dancing with it.

Chango / Shango / Xango / Sango

Purpose: Fourth King of the Yoruba, immortalized as the God of Thunder, Power, Victory

Corresponding saints: Saint Barbara, Saint Jerome

Prayer to Saint Barbara

O Glorious St. Barbara, you inspire me by your example of courage and chastity. Help me to have your gift of faith, and obtain for me, through your prayers, the grace to live a holy life, so that one day I may join you in the Kingdom of Heaven.

Amen

St. Barbara, Pray for Us!

Ogun / Ogum

Ogun is the God of Metals, Minerals, Tools, War, Birds, and Wild Beasts

Purpose: Gives work to the Unemployed, Protector, Warrior

Corresponding saints: Saint John the Baptist, Saint Anthony of Padua, Saint George, San Pedro (Saint Simon Peter),

Here is a prayer to use when working with your Ogun Voodoo doll:

Litany of Saint Anthony of Padua

Lord, have mercy on us.

Christ, have mercy on us.

Lord, have mercy on us.

Christ, hear us.

Christ, graciously hear us.

God, the Father of Heaven, have mercy on us.

God, the Son, Redeemer of the world, have mercy on us.

God, the Holy Spirit, have mercy on us.

Holy Trinity, one God, have mercy on us.

Holy Mary,

Saint Anthony of Padua,

Saint Anthony, glory of the Friars Minor,

Saint Anthony, ark of the testament,

Saint Anthony, sanctuary of heavenly wisdom,

Saint Anthony, destroyer of worldly vanity,

Saint Anthony, conqueror of impurity,

Saint Anthony, example of humility,

Saint Anthony, lover of the Cross,

Saint Anthony, martyr of desire,

Saint Anthony, generator of charity,

Saint Anthony, zealous for justice,

Saint Anthony, terror of infidels,

Saint Anthony, model of perfection,

Saint Anthony, consoler of the afflicted,

Saint Anthony, restorer of lost things,

Saint Anthony, defender of innocence,

Saint Anthony, liberator of prisoners,

Saint Anthony, guide of pilgrims,

Saint Anthony, restorer of health.

Saint Anthony, performer of miracles,

Saint Anthony, restorer of speech to the mute,

Saint Anthony, restorer of hearing to the deaf,

Saint Anthony, restorer of sight to the blind,

Saint Anthony, disperser of devils,

Saint Anthony, reviver of the dead.

Saint Anthony, tamer of tyrants,

From the snares of the devil, Saint Anthony deliver us.

From thunder, lightning, and storms, Saint Anthony deliver us.

From all evil of body and soul, Saint Anthony deliver us.

Through your intercession, Saint Anthony protect us.

Throughout the course of life, Saint Anthony protect us.

Lamb of God, who takes away the sins of the world, spare us, O Lord.

Lamb of God, who takes away the sins of the world, graciously hear us, O Lord.

Lamb of God, who takes away the sins of the world, have mercy on us.

V. Saint Anthony, pray for us.

R. That we may be made worthy of the promises of Christ.

O my God, may the pious commemoration of Saint Anthony, your Confessor and Proctor, give joy to your Church, that she may ever be strengthened with your spiritual assistance and merit to attain everlasting joy. Through Christ our Lord. Amen.

Orunla/ Orunmila/Orula

Purpose: Teacher, Prophet

Corresponding saints: Saint John the Evangelist taking Jesus down from cross

Prayer to Saint John the Evangelist

O Glorious Saint John, you were so loved by Jesus that you merited to rest your head upon his breast, and to be left in his place as a son to Mary. Obtain for us an ardent love for Jesus and Mary. Let me be united with them now on earth and forever after in heaven. Amen.

Babalú-Ayé

Purpose: Spirit of Disease and Sickness, also Provider of Money to the Poor

Corresponding saint: Saint Lazarus of Dives

Prayer to Saint Lazarus

Dear Patron and assistant to the poor and sick, with this prayer I request your assistance, and with the aid of the Holy Spirit may the Lord always protect me during sickness and in health. St. Lazarus, give me the strength to overcome all the temptations on earth, in the name of the Father, the Son, and the Holy Spirit. Amen.

General Prayers

Here are some general prayers to use when working with your Voodoo doll. These prayers are commonly used in Voodoo rituals.

Our Father

Our Father, who art in Heaven, hallowed be Thy name.
Thy kingdom come. Thy will be done on earth as it is in heaven.
Give us this day our daily bread; and, forgive us our trespasses
as we forgive those who trespass against us.
And, lead us not into temptation. And, deliver us from evil.
For the kingdom, the power and the glory are yours now and forever. Amen.

Hail Mary

Hail Mary, full of grace, the Lord is with Thee.
Blessed are Thou amongst women and blessed is the fruit of Thy womb, Jesus.
Holy Mary, Mother of God, pray for us sinners, now and at the hour of our death.
Amen.

Apostle's Creed

We believe in one God, the Father, the Almighty, Creator of heaven and Earth, of all that is seen and unseen.

We believe in his son, Jesus Christ, who was born of the Virgin Mary, suffered under Pontius Pilate, was crucified, died and was buried. He descended into hell.

One the third day, He rose again, in fulfillment of the scriptures. He is seated at the right hand of the Father where His kingdom will have no end.

We believe in one holy catholic and apostolic church. We acknowledge one baptism for the forgiveness of sins. We look to the resurrection of the dead and life everlasting.

Amen.

Prayer to the Seven African Powers

Oh, Seven African Powers, who are so close to our divine Savior,

With great humility I kneel before thee and implore your intercession before the Great Spirit.

Hear my petition and grant me peace and prosperity.

Please remove all of the obstacles that cause me to stray from the Beauty Way.

Oh Olofi, I trust in the words "ask and you shall receive". Let it be so!

Amen.

(Make your petition)

CHAPTER 13:
Cursed Voodoo Dolls

Not everyone who believes they have been cursed or hoodooed actually has been. To find out if you have been hoodooed, you should have a divination done by a reputable practitioner, or do a divination yourself using cards, a pendulum, or some other divination system with which you are familiar. The results of the divination will reveal whether or not your situation is due to being crossed or jinxed.

If the misfortune you are experiencing is not due to a medical or mental health condition, and you are certain it is due to some unwanted spiritual force, then you should take steps to reverse it. It helps to know who has crossed you, and it helps if you have the object with which you have been cursed so that you can destroy it.

What Does a Cursed Voodoo Doll Look Like?

You have found an unusual looking doll on your doorstep or in your parking garage at work. You get a creepy feeling just looking at it. Come to think of it, you have had a streak of bad luck lately. Was this doll put there for you to find? Is someone sending you a message on the down low?

Voodoo Dolls

A person who wants to lay a trick on you can use any type of doll they wish. It does not have to be the stereotypical ugly Voodoo doll with some of your personal effects attached to it. Sometimes, it can be as innocent looking as a sweet baby doll that is the object of any little girl's affection.

For example, below is a picture of a Voodoo doll that was put in the path of someone at their place of employment. It was strategically placed in the parking lot facing the individual's car. It looks like one of those Brat dolls you can find in any department store. But how would you know it is carrying a curse?

Photo: 59. Cursed Voodoo doll.

Cursed Voodoo Dolls

Well, the first clue is rather obvious - her face is painted black. This is a good indication that it is a tool in someone's ritual work. I mean, they don't come with their faces painted black, do they?

Secondly, she has no feet. This is another indication that this doll may have been intentionally altered to lay a curse on someone. Painting the face black and removing the feet are both consistent with the general principle of using shocking images to psych out an intended target. Also, what is done to the doll can be viewed as a metaphor for what is intended for the victim. For example, removing the feet is consistent with restraining and rendering a person immobile.

Below is another doll that was believed to be cursed. In this case, the doll bride represented the daughter-in-law of the person casting the spell. At first glance, she seems like a beautiful baby doll. But upon removing her veil, it became evident that her hair had been clipped off, and looking under her dress, her feet had been removed.

Photo: 60. Cursed bride Voodoo doll.

How to Get Rid of a Cursed Voodoo Doll

If you have been given a Voodoo doll and you sense it carries negativity, and you are confident in your ability to confront a Voodoo hex or curse, then follow these instructions for getting rid of a cursed Voodoo doll:

Wrap the cursed doll or object in a white cloth and sprinkle it generously with sea salt. Take it to a river or stream or far away from your home deep in the woods. Bring an offering of fruit and some coins and ask the spirits of the water or the trees to take the negative energy and transform it through the power of the earth and water. Toss it into the water along with the offerings or bury it under a tree with the offerings. Walk away without looking back. When you return home, light a 7-day protection candle and take a bath with cleansing herbs and sea salt.

Another way to get rid of a cursed Voodoo doll is to do the following:

On a Saturday, place the doll or object in a clean white cloth. Take it somewhere far away from your home and find a tree. Dig a hole in the earth at the base of the tree. Place the cloth wrapped doll in the hole and burn it. Then, cover the remaining ashes with Holy Water and cover the hole over with the dirt. The earth will transform the dark energy into light and blessings. When you return home, light a 7-day protection candle and take a bath with cleansing herbs and sea salt, or add some Holy Water to your bath.

Here's a purification bath you can take after getting rid of a negative Voodoo doll:

White Bath for Purification

This is good for when you feel spiritually dirty, feel the need to cleanse your aura, need spiritual revitalization, or for cold and flu symptoms.

First, light a white or red candle and burn either coconut or blessings incense. Add the following to your bath water:

2 to 4 cups of evaporated milk or powdered milk

2 to 4 tablespoons of anise

Wash with sea salt.

Voodoo Doll Reversal Spells

If you are wondering what to do when someone has sent some negative energy your way via a spell, curse, jinx, hex, or crossing, follow these instructions. Procure a general purpose Voodoo doll. Write the person's name on a piece of parchment paper, anoint with olive oil, and tuck into the doll. Burn a white candle on a Saturday, under the waning moon, as you chant the following again and again: "All harmful intent you meant for me returns to you (insert person's name) times three!!!" In this way, you are simply acting as a "mirror," reflecting all the negativity back to the original sender. The person will receive back what he/she has sent out three-fold.

Another way to reverse a curse is to create a Voodoo doll or poppet to represent the person who has cursed you. Place the doll in a wooden box and bury it in a shallow hole under a thin layer of dirt. Make a large fire over the spot where the doll is buried and chant the following:

Voodoo Dolls

May the curse that was placed against me be consumed with the flames that burn this doll. May the evil intentions of the one who has cursed be transformed with the energy of the sacred fire into that which is harmless.

CHAPTER 14:
Recipes for Magickal Oils

The following are some of the recipes for the oils and powders used in the spells in this book. These oils and powders can be purchased, which is probably the easiest way to procure them for most folks. However, if you are so inclined, have a go at it making them yourself.

Bend-Over Oil

This extremely potent oil makes other people do your bidding. Use it to break any hexes and to order evil spirits to return to their sender. This oil is suitable for anointing candles and Voodoo dolls.

Calamus root
Licorice root
Bergamot leaf or essential oil of bergamot

Blend together with a few grains of frankincense in almond oil.

Black Arts Oil

There are many recipes for Black Arts Oil. Here's a quick one:

half a dropper essential oil of patchouli
half a dropper essential oil of black pepper
a pinch of valerian root
a pinch of black poodle dog hair
a pinch of black mustard seeds
a pinch of Spanish moss
a pinch of mullein
a pinch of mastic
a pinch of powdered sulphur
nine whole black peppercorns

Blend into one half-ounce carrier oil such as almond. Oil will be dark brown in color.

Command and Compel Oil

In a base of mineral oil, blend the following ingredients:

> Essential oil of bergamot
> Licorice root
> Calamus root
> Few bits of frankincense
> Top off with honeysuckle or rose oil for fragrance

Allow the mixture to steep for 30 days in a cool dark place. Then, you can use as is or strain it into another container.

Crossing Oil

Appropriate for anointing dolls and candles for the purpose of curses and hexes. Mix equal amounts of wormwood and pepperwort. Of this mixture put two tablespoons in two ounces of oil. Add a small piece of ground ivy root.

Crossing Powder

Blend sulphur, graveyard dirt, cayenne pepper, and ground ivy leaves. Add rattlesnake skin if you are lucky enough to find it.

Fast Luck Oil

Blend oil of cinnamon, oil of vanilla, and oil of wintergreen. Add to a base of almond or grapeseed oil with a few drops of vitamin E oil, and toss in a few flakes of alkanet to make the oil red, and some crushed pyrite (Fool's Gold) to enhance its money drawing effect.

Revenge Oil

Revenge Oil is used to seek revenge against one who has done you a great wrong. For this oil you will need:

Red Pepper
Sulfur
Wormwood

Voodoo Dolls

Ground ivy root

Add equal amounts of each to two ounces of base oil.

Final Thoughts

As I sit and write my final thoughts about this book, I can't help but reflect on some of the issues raised in the process. Everything is so much more than what it seems; what is a child's toy to one person, is a sacred vessel to another. What seems to be a harmless marketing ploy, is a stab in the very soul of another.

I hope that the skeptical reader will see that Voodoo dolls are not the objects of Satan and devil worshippers, nor are they to be used for the purpose of harming another. They are a continuation of ancient religious practices, as well as an extension of an age old human tendency to seek personal empowerment in times of great difficulty.

The stereotypes associated with Voodoo dolls in contemporary society are problematic; however, the dolls themselves are not. The relationship an individual has with any object is the issue; the responsibility lays with the person who creates and possesses the object and ultimately, what they choose to do with it.

Hopefully, you have found the tutorials in this book to be useful and inspiring. I encourage you to be creative with your doll making, make them into objects of endearment, and use them to help you accomplish your goals in life and for connecting with the Divine. Voodoo dolls are nothing new; they are simply an adapted traditional and sacred art form. Let's keep them that way.

May our ancestors guide and protect your every step!

Suppliers

All of the Voodoo dolls, herbs, oils, candles and such that are mentioned in this book can be obtained from spiritual supply stores and botanicas. Here are a few reputable stores that I recommend that also have websites for your convenience.

The Mystic Voodoo
501 E 6th St. West Liberty, IA. 52776
Hours of operation: 9 AM to 5PM CST Monday through Friday, closed weekends. Orders can be placed 24 hours a day, 7 days a week.
Email: mysticvoodoo@mysticvoodoo.com
Order online: www.mysticvoodoo.com
Website description: The Mystic Voodoo specializes in authentic, hand crafted Voodoo dolls, spiritual jewelry, and metaphysical books and ebooks.

New Orleans Mistic
P.O. Box 740516
New Orleans, LA 70174
1-504-218-5305

Voodoo Dolls

Hours of operation: 10 AM - 3 PM CST Monday through Friday. They are closed weekends.

Email: tribble@neworleansmistic.com

Order online: http://www.neworleansmistic.com/main.htm

Description: New Orleans Mistic is a mail order spiritual supply that has been serving customers since 1990.

Lucky Mojo Curio Co.

6632 Covey Road

Forestville, California 95436

Phone: 707-887-1521

Fax: 707-887-7128

Email: order@luckymojo.com

Hours of operation: Open 7 Days a Week, 9:00 am - 5:00 pm Pacific Time

Order online: http://www.luckymojo.com/catalogue.html

Website description: "We have about 3500 different herbs, roots, candles, dressing oils and ritual oils, essential oils, incense blends, amulets, books, tarot and cartomancy cards, mineral curios, posters, holy cards, religious statues, soaps, hair care products, zoological curios, and crystal salts in stock at any given time, but if you want particular items custom-made for you, please phone us ahead so that we can put them together in time for your arrival, or be prepared to watch (and even pitch in!) as we prepare your order to your specifications."

Wisdom Products

16927 S. Main St. Suite B

Gardena, CA 90248

Phone: 310-327-2184

Fax: 562-453-3348

Email: customerservice@wisdomproducts.net

Hours of operation: 8:00 AM - 4:00 PM (Pacific time) Monday – Friday

Order online: www.wisdomproducts.net

Website description: "You will find a wide variety of quality items to supply your spiritual and new age needs". English/Spanish.

Bibliography

Alvarado, D. (2008) *The Voodoo Hoodoo Spellbook*. West Liberty, IA: The Mystic Voodoo.

Ankarloo, B., Flint, V. I. J., Clark, S., Cryer, F. H., Thomsen, M. (1999). *Witchcraft and Magic in Europe: Ancient Greece and Rome*. University of Pennsylvania Press

Bleier, S. P. (1995). *African Vodun: Art, Psychology, and Power*. Chicago and London: The University of Chicago Press.

Bleier, S. P. (1993). "Truth and Seeing: Magic, Custom and Fetish in Art History." In *Africa and the Disciplines: The Contributions of Research in Africa to the Social Sciences and Humanities*, Robert H. Bates, V. Y. Mudimbe, Jean F. O'Barr, Ed.s. Chicago: University of Chicago Press.

Brandstötter, S. (n.d.) *Voodoo in New Orleans*, Retrieved from: http://angam.ang.univie.ac.at/LiveMiss/Voodoo/index.htm

Cameron, E. (1996). *Isn't S/He a Doll? Play and Ritual in African Sculpture*. Los Angeles: UCLA Fowler Museum of Cultural History.

Charles, J. (2003). *Vodou's Veil*. Retrieved from: http://www.hartford-hwp.com/archives/43a/525.html

Cosentino, D. (1998). *Vodou Things: The Art of Pierrot Barra and Marie Cassaise*. Jackson MS: UP of Mississippi.

Bibliography

Cosentino, D, ed. (1995). *Sacred Arts of Haitian Vodou*. Los Angeles: UCLA Fowler Museum.

Dagan, E. A. (1990). *African Dolls for Play & Magic*. Montreal: Galerie Amrad African Arts.

Faraone, C. A. (1991) Binding and Burying the Forces of Evil: The Defensive Use of 'Voodoo Dolls' in Ancient Greece, *Classical Antiquity*, *10*, 2, pp. 165-205.

Faraone, C. A. (1988). *Talismans, Voodoo dolls in ancient Greece*, Stanford.

Green, Y. (1997). *African Girl and Boy Paper Dolls*. New York: Dover Publications, Inc.

Lang, A. (1900). Fetishism and Spiritualism, *The Making of Religion*, (Chapter VIII), Longmans, Green, and C: London, New York and Bombay, pp. 147-159.

Larson, J. L. (1995). *Folk Art from the Global Village*. Santa Fe, NM: Museum of New Mexico Press.

Lipsitz, George. 1995. "Diasporic Intimacy in the art of Renée Stout." *Dear Robert, I'll See You at the Crossroads" A Project by Renée Stout*. Seattle and London: University of Washington Press.

MacGaffey, Wyatt. 1993. "The Eyes of Understanding: Kongo *minkisi*." *Astonishment and Power*. Washington and London: Smithsonian Institution Press.

McAlister, Elizabeth. 1995. "A Sorcerer's Bottle." *Sacred Arts of the Haitian Vodou*. Los Angeles: Fowler Museum of Cultural History.

Morin, R. (2006). Who do that Voodoo at Harvard? *Pew Research Center Publications*. Retrieved: http://pewresearch.org/pubs/66/who-do-that-voodoo-at-harvard

Negri, S. (1993). Kachina Carving Artistry in Wood. *Arizona Highways*, pp. 15-17.

Voodoo Dolls

Nemser, Cindy. (1975). *Art Talk: Conversations with Fifteen Women Artists.* New York: Icon Editions.

Welch, J. D. (2008). *Constructing Power: Assemblage and Personal Empowerment.* Retrieved from: http://www.jdwelch.net/writing/assemblage.html

Wright, B. (1977). *Kachinas.* Flagstaff, Az. Northland Press, 1977.

http://www.portcult.com/SAINT_CYPRIAN.05.MAGIC.SPELLS.htm

Printed in France by Amazon
Brétigny-sur-Orge, FR